# IS BEHAVIORAL ECONOMICS
# DOOMED?

**David K. Levine** is John H. Biggs Distinguished Professor of Economics at Washington University in St. Louis. He is currently serving as President of the Society for the Advancement of Economic Theory. He is also a fellow of the Econometric Society, an Economic Theory Fellow, a research associate of the NBER, and of the Federal Reserve Bank of St. Louis, managing editor of *NAJ Economics*, and co-director of the MISSEL laboratory. His scientific research is supported by grants from the National Science Foundation. He is the author of *Against Intellectual Monopoly* (with Michele Boldrin) and *Learning in Games* (with Drew Fudenberg) and the editor of several conference volumes. He has published extensively in professional journals, including *The American Economic Review, Econometrica, The Review of Economic Studies, The Journal of Political Economy, The Journal of Economic Theory, The Quarterly Journal of Economics*, and *The American Political Science Review*. Levine's current research interests include the study of intellectual property and endogenous growth in dynamic general equilibrium models, models of self-control, of the endogenous formation of preferences, institutions and social norms, learning in games, evolutionary game theory, virtual economies, and the application of game theory to experimental economics. At the graduate level, his teaching focuses on economic dynamics; at the undergraduate level, he teaches intermediate level microeconomics, focusing largely on elementary game theory.

# IS BEHAVIORAL ECONOMICS DOOMED?

*The Ordinary versus the Extraordinary*

Edited by

David K. Levine

# OpenBook Publishers

Open Book Publishers CIC Ltd.,
40 Devonshire Road, Cambridge, CB1 2BL, United Kingdom
http://www.openbookpublishers.com

As with all Open Book Publishers titles, digital material and resources
associated with this volume are available from our website:
http://www.openbookpublishers.com/product/77

ISBN Hardback: 978-1-906924-93-5
ISBN Paperback: 978-1-906924-92-8
ISBN Digital (pdf): 978-1-906924-94-2
ISBN e-book (epub): 978-1-906924-95-9
ISBN e-book (mobi): 978-1-906924-96-6

Cover image: Joan M. Mas
http://www.flickr.com/photos/dailypic/2072852387/in/photostream
Typesetting by www.bookgenie.in

All paper used by Open Book Publishers is SFI (Sustainable Forestry
Initiative), PEFC (Programme for the Endorsement of Forest Certification
Schemes) and Forest Stewardship Council (FSC) certified.

Printed in the United Kingdom and United States by
Lightning Source for Open Book Publishers

# Contents

|  | Page |
|---|---|
| Acknowledgements | vii |
| Introduction | 1 |
| Does Economic Theory Work? | 5 |
| Why Is the World so Irrational? | 21 |
| Does Economic Theory Fail? | 47 |
| You Can Fool Some of the People... | 63 |
| Behavioral Theories I: Biases and Irrationality | 77 |
| Behavioral Theories II: Time and Uncertainty | 93 |
| Learning and Friends | 111 |
| Conclusion: Psychology, Neuroscience and Economics | 123 |
| References | 131 |
| Index | 139 |

*To Milena Davidson-Levine and Catharina Tilmans*

# Acknowledgements

I owe an immeasurable intellectual debt to my coauthors Michele Boldrin, Drew Fudenberg, Salvatore Modica, Zacharias Maniadis, Tom Palfrey, and Jie Zheng with whom I've worked, discussed and debated the issues discussed here for many years. Tim Sullivan encouraged me to write this up in the form of a book, and took the time to read and comment on the first draft. Rupert Gatti, economics editor of Open Book Publishers, Alessandra Tosi and two exceptional referees have enormously improved that original draft. Juan Block proofread the book – for sense as well as typos – and provided the index.

This book originated as a Max Weber lecture presented at the European University Institute. Much of it was written while on sabbatical leave in the Economics Department there. I am grateful to the EUI and the Economics Department. I also owe a special debt of gratitude to the Max Weber program and to Ramon Marimon, Karin Tilmans and the Weber fellows for the invitation to speak, for a very constructive presentation, and for encouragement and assistance in writing up the lecture.

I have presented variations of this lecture in various venues including FUR, the NYU Experimental Workshop, the Neuroeconomics Meetings and the Milan Neuroeconomics Conference. I am grateful to Glenn Harrison, Guillame Frechette, and Colin Camerer for those invitations and to them and the meeting participants for helpful comments and criticism. Like Guillame and Colin, Rosemarie Nagel disagrees with practically everything written here – but her constant provocation has resulted in a much more coherent book. In the other dimension – Charlie Plott's work in a direction similar to mine has been an example and an inspiration.

Although we may disagree – hopefully with respect – I could not have written this book without my many behavioral, neuroscientific and psychological friends. George Ainslie, Gary Charness, Ernst Fehr, Paul

Glimcher, Len Green, Joel Myerson, David Laibson, Camillo Padoa-Schioppa, Drazen Prelec, Aldo Rustichini and Klaus Schmidt have through their careful research contributed to my understanding of behavioral economics.

I am also grateful to my daughter Milena Davidson-Levine, to Catharina Tilmans and to my many students both graduate and undergraduate at Washington University in St. Louis. To the outstanding faculty there and the fine research organization at the Federal Reserve Bank of St. Louis I am also indebted for constant feedback and support.

Finally, I would like to thank the National Science Foundation and grants SES-03-14713 and SES-08-51315 for financial support.

# 1. Introduction

*Under these conditions, the erotic relation seems to offer the unsurpassable peak of the fulfillment of the request for love in the direct fusion of the souls of one to the other. The boundless giving of oneself is as radical as possible in its opposition to all functionality, rationality, and generality. It is so overpowering that it is treated "symbolically": as a sacrament. The lover realizes himself to be rooted in the kernel of the truly living, which is eternally inaccessible to any rational endeavor. He knows himself to be freed from the cold skeleton hands of rational orders, just as completely as from the banality of everyday routine.* Max Weber, 1958

Even Max Weber – one of the early proponents of the social analysis of rational man – recognized the essential irrationality of emotions such as love. Today it has become so very fashionable to criticize economic theory for focusing too much on rationality and ignoring the imperfect and emotional way in which decisions are reached in the "real world." Psychologists and other social scientists have been especially vocal in their dismay. A bright new group of behavioral economists has picked up the criticism:

> Economics traditionally conceptualizes a world populated by calculating, unemotional maximizers that have been dubbed Homo economicus. The standard economic framework ignores or rules out virtually all the behavior studied by cognitive and social psychologists. This "unbehavioral" economic agent was once defended on numerous grounds: some claimed that the model was "right"; most others simply argued that the standard model was easier to formalize and practically more relevant. Behavioral economics blossomed from the realization that neither point of view was correct. (Thaler and Mullainathan, 2010)

The authors go on to point out how modern economics is based on a foundation of sand.

> The standard economic model of human behavior includes three unrealistic traits – unbounded rationality, unbounded willpower, and unbounded selfishness – all of which behavioral economics modifies.

Those who have read about – and who has not? – the current economic crisis may wonder indeed just how rational an economic man or woman might be. Behavioral economics has become the modern rage. Is, therefore, rational economic man – *homo economicus* – dead? Has the economics profession moved on to recognize the true irrationality of humankind? Nothing could be further from the truth.

Strangely, the criticisms that have caused behavioral economics to blossom are nothing new. Writing in 1898 Thorstein Veblen wrote sarcastically of rational economic man as

> a lightning calculator of pleasures and pains, who oscillates like a homogenous globule of desire of happiness under the impulse of stimuli.

Students of economic history can argue about whether Veblen's description of *homo economicus* is an accurate reflection of economics as it was practiced then – it is definitely not an accurate reflection of economics as it is practiced today. For starters, while mainstream economics does indeed presume unlimited self-control, it does not presume unlimited rationality or unbounded selfishness. The paradigmatic man (or more often these days woman) in modern economics is that of a decision-maker beset on all sides by uncertainty. Most important, the central focus of economics is on how successful we are in coming to grips with that uncertainty.

Remarkably, for a long period of time during the 1960s and 1970s, irrational economic man dominated economics. It was the abysmal failures of the "neoclassical synthesis" leading to absurd and costly failures of economic policy – I am old enough to remember waiting in long lines to buy gasoline – that led to the modern and much-criticized theory of rational expectations. The fact is that irrational economic man is a poorer description of how we behave than that of a "lightning calculator of pleasures and pains." As Robert Lucas wrote in 1995, in many ways the rational expectations model was a reaction to

> [t]he implicit presumption in these... models [of irrational man]... that people could be fooled over and over again.

Modern economics is not the theory imagined by critics – including apparently some Nobel Prize winning economists – who are unfamiliar with it. The theory used by working economists is far more sophisticated and successful than is generally imagined. The fact that policy makers choose to ignore our warnings does not make us wrong. Weaknesses in economic analysis exist – but bear little connection to those cited by critics.

My objective in this volume is to set the record straight by explaining some of the true successes and failures of both economics and behavioral economics.

To understand whether or not behavioral economics is doomed is to first ask the question whether mainstream economics has failed. If it has not, then surely behavioral economics is doomed. And mainstream economics has not failed. Existing economic theory in those situations of greatest interest to economists makes strong and robust predictions. Those predictions are borne out by the facts – in the laboratory as well as in the field.

In some situations less central to economics the theory makes weak predictions. These are also borne out by the facts – but the theory is less useful as it fails to narrow down the range of possibilities. It is here – in strengthening existing theory – that there exists a potential for behavioral ideas. Indeed – long before the term "behavioral economics" existed – many of the ideas discussed by "behavioral economists" had already been incorporated into mainstream economic models. Here I will tell the story of both the successes and failures.

"Wait!" you say. Does not the inability of economists to forecast the current economic crisis show that all you claim is false? How can you defend a science that has met with such an abysmal failure? In response I ask – do you condemn quantum mechanics as useless because it cannot predict simultaneously the location and velocity of subatomic particles? Because not only can it not do so – according to the theory it is impossible for it to do so. Just so: according to economic theory – for reasons I will elucidate – it is equally impossible to predict the timing of economic crises. Does that make us useless? If we can – and we certainly can – tell how economic crises can be avoided, how they can be mitigated, and how best to recover from them – then surely you ought to listen to what I have to say.

# 2. Does Economic Theory Work?

It is impossible to have an intelligent discussion of economics, of game theory, or of behavioral economics – let alone their successes and failures – without some idea of what they are about. *Homo economicus* is a far different creature than commonly imagined. Let us begin by examining this mythical construct more closely.

## What is Game Theory?

The heart of modern "rational" economic theory is the concept of a non-cooperative or "Nash" equilibrium of a game. If you saw the movie *A Beautiful Mind* this theory – created by Nobel Laureate John Nash – is briefly described, albeit inaccurately. But to put the oxen before the cart, let us first describe what a *game* is. A game in the parlance of a game theorist or economist does not generally refer to a parlor game such as checkers or bridge, nor indeed to Super-Mario III. Instead, what economists call game theory psychologists more accurately call the theory of social situations. There are two branches of game theory, but the one most widely used in economics is the theory of non-cooperative games – I shall describe that theory here.

The central topic of non-cooperative game theory is the question of how people interact. A game in the formal sense used by economists is merely a careful description of a social situation specifying the options available to the "players," how choices among those options result in "outcomes," and how the participants "feel" about those outcomes. The timing of decisions and the information available to players when undertaking those decisions must also be described.

The critical element in analyzing what happens in a game (or social situation) is the beliefs of the players: what do they think is likely to happen? How do they think other players are likely to play? From a formalistic perspective the beliefs of players are generally described by probability distributions – we assign a probability to an outcome – although in more advanced theories – such as epistemic game theory – beliefs are more sophisticated and mathematically complicated objects. Please observe that the notion that we are uncertain about the world we live in and about the people we interact with is at the very core of game theory.

Given beliefs about consequences and sentiments about those outcomes it is almost tautological to postulate that players choose the most favorable course of action given their beliefs. At one level this is what it means for players to be "rational" and should scarcely be controversial... yet many dense books have been written criticizing this notion of rationality.

Of course a theory that says that players believe something and do the best they can based on those beliefs is an empty theory because it does not say where beliefs come from. I sell my stocks? I must believe the market is going down. I spend all my money? I must believe the world is coming to an end. And so forth. The formation of beliefs is at the center of modern economic theory.

Our beliefs surely depend on what we know. I believe that if I drop this computer it will fall to the ground – because I have a lifetime of experience with falling objects. By way of contrast I have no idea when I wake up tomorrow morning whether the stock market will have gone up or down, and even less what might be the consequences of clean coal technology for global warming over the next decade.

Historically the economics profession has been most interested in situations where the players are experienced. For example, investment decisions are typically made by investors with long and deep experience of investment opportunities; most transactions are concluded between buyers and sellers with much experience in buying and selling. Under these circumstances it is natural to imagine that beliefs reflect underlying realities. In the theory of competitive markets this has been called rational expectations. In game theory it is called Nash equilibrium. Notice, however, that such a theory does not demand that people know the future – we call that "perfect foresight" not "rational expectations" – only that the probabilities they assign to the future are the same probabilities shared by other equally experienced individuals. Put differently: while I have no idea whether when I wake up tomorrow morning the stock market will have gone up or down, I do know that both outcomes are about equally likely. As this view is widely shared, it represents "rational expectations" about tomorrow's stock prices.

Another way to describe Nash equilibrium is this: Nash equilibrium represents a setting in which no further learning is possible. That is – if some player holds wrong beliefs the possibility exists that they will discover their mistake and learn something new. When possibilities for learning are exhausted what we find is Nash equilibrium.

How well does the theory of Nash equilibrium work? One of the most widely used empirical tools in modern behavioral economics is the laboratory experiment in which paid participants – many times college undergraduates, but often other groups from diverse ethnic and social backgrounds – are brought together to interact in artificially created social situations to study how they reach decisions individually or in groups. Many anomalies with theory have been discovered in the laboratory – and rightfully these are given emphasis among practitioners – we are, after all more interested in strengthening the weaknesses in our theories than in simply repeating that they are correct. Amidst all this the basic fact should not be lost that standard economic theory works remarkably well in the laboratory.

Let me be more specific. Let us take as our theory the theory of Nash equilibrium. Let us also suppose (we will talk more about this later) that laboratory subjects care only about bringing home the most possible money from the experiment. Do we observe Nash equilibrium in the laboratory?

# Voting

One of the most controversial applications of the theory of rational man is to voting. Modern voting theory, for example the 1996 theory of Feddersen and Pesendorfer, is based on the idea that your vote only matters when it decides an election – when your vote is *pivotal*. This has implications for voter participation. If elections are not close there is no chance of your vote mattering, and no incentive to participate. To be an equilibrium, elections must be so close that the chance of changing the outcome is enough to compensate for the cost of participating. Whether this is how voters behave is quite controversial: it is often referred to as "the paradox of voter turnout." It is central to Green and Shapiro's harsh 1994 critique of rational choice theory in which they assert that

> Those tests that have been undertaken [of rational choice theory] have either failed on their own terms or garnered theoretical support for propositions that, on reflection, can only be characterized as banal: they do little more than restate existing knowledge in rational choice terminology.

In 2007 Levine and Palfrey examined voter participation in the laboratory. Our subjects were UCLA (University of California, Los Angeles) undergraduates. After arrival at the laboratory the subjects were divided into unequal teams of voters. Later, various elections were conducted: in some elections one "party" had a 2/3rds majority, in others a one-vote majority. We conducted elections with numbers of participants ranging from three to fifty-one.

In these elections voters had a choice between casting a vote for their own party and abstaining. Voters received a small payment for participating in the experiment plus the members of each winning party received a prize of $0.37 each. This was split between the two parties in case of a tie. Voting in the laboratory – as in real life – was costly. Each voter was randomly assigned a cost of voting ranging from $0.00 to $0.185. This cost was known only to the voter to whom it was assigned – all other aspects of the experiment were commonly known to all the voters.

Notice that in this setup the most you can hope to do is to swing a losing election to a tie, or swing a tie to a win, in either case garnering an additional $0.185. So if you drew the lowest voting cost of $0.00 it makes sense to vote as long as there is even a small chance of changing the outcome, while if you drew the highest cost of $0.185 you would never vote unless you were absolutely certain to change the outcome. For other costs whether it is a good idea to participate or not depends on how likely you think you are to alter the outcome. For instance, if you think the probability of influencing the election is high you should accept a higher cost of voting.

Sticking with the (not entirely plausible) assumption that voters are strict moneygrubbers, it is possible but not easy to compute the Nash equilibrium of this game. Depending on the probability of making a difference there is a threshold cost below which it is rational to vote, and above which it is not – this is known as a "cut-off" decision. The participation rate is determined by this threshold – the higher the threshold, the higher the participation rate. Conversely the higher the participation rate, the less likely it is that voters make a difference. This kind of interdependence is described by economists and mathematicians as a fixed-point problem, and requires solving – in this case – some rather complex non-linear equations. This can be done only on the computer, and while in principle there could be more than one solution to these equations, in fact there is only one. Thus using the computer we made this difficult calculation determining for each election what was the Nash equilibrium.

As indicated, we then re-created the theoretical environment in the laboratory. We had no expectation that voters could guess, calculate, or otherwise intuitively figure out how best to behave – as I mentioned it is quite a complex problem. Rather, as is central to modern economic theory (see the quote of Lucas above), we imagined that if voters were given an opportunity to learn they would reach an equilibrium. Hence, we gave them ample opportunity to learn – voters got to participate in fifty elections each.

To measure how well the theory worked we focused on how likely it was for a player to make a difference. A pivotal event in this experiment is a situation that is either a tie, or one party wins by a single vote. Since voters only participate because they have a chance of being pivotal, in equilibrium the chance of such an event cannot be too small. Since elections "often" have to be close, it follows that there must also be upsets in which the minority party wins. The theory also predicts how frequently this will occur. For each type of election we computed what was the probability of pivotal events and upsets. For those of you familiar with social science research, you should notice what we did not do. We did not collect a bunch of data about behavior and fit a curve to it and declare that our curve "fits the data well" or is "statistically significant." We did not declare that if there are more voters the participation rate should be "lower." For any election with any number of voters, and any size of prizes and probabilities of drawing participation costs the theory of Nash equilibrium makes precise quantitative predictions about the frequency with which we should observe elections results that are pivotal and elections that result in an upset.

What happened with real people in our experimental laboratory? The figure below shows the results on a graph in which the horizontal axis has the frequencies we computed from the theory of Nash equilibrium and the vertical axis has the corresponding frequencies of actual election results in the laboratory. Each different election setting with different numbers of voters in each party corresponds to a different point on the graph. If the theory worked perfectly all of these points should lie on the 45 degree line where the theory exactly matches the data – for instance if the theory predicts 0.4 then we should observe 0.4. As you can clearly see – that is exactly what happens – the theory works more or less perfectly. If you do not believe this, try dropping tennis balls out your window and calculating the force of gravity and see how accurate your measurement is. Less good than this I can assure you.

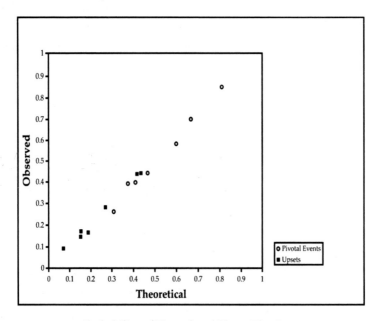

Probability of Pivotal and Upset Elections

Let us again emphasize what we did not do. Often when social scientists say their theory fits the data what they mean is that they "estimated free parameters" and given their best estimate of those parameters the corresponding model reflects the data. This would be as if instead of saying that our observations should lie on the 45 degree line, we said they should lie on some unknown line – the slope and intercept of that line being "free parameters" – and declaring victory if we could find a line that more or less passed through the data. Here there are no free parameters; nothing is estimated, there are no unknowns. We take the information about the setting – how many voters; what prizes, and so forth – and we calculate a number – the probability of a pivotal event or upset using the sharp predictions of Nash equilibrium. This number is then either right or wrong – in fact it is right. But there is no wiggle room to "estimate parameters" or otherwise fudge around with things.

# Economics is a Quantitative Subject

The voting experiment illustrates what economics is and what it is not. It is not about the intersection of supply and demand curves, and about what direction prices move if a curve "shifts." It is a quantitative theory of human behavior both individually and in interaction with other people.

The importance of the quantitative nature of economics often eludes clever observers, especially philosophers and lawyers. Take for example the following (possibly apocryphal) quotation – from the "original" behavioral economist Kenneth Boulding

> anyone who believes exponential growth can go on forever in a finite world is either a madman or an economist.

This appears to involve a straw man, since as far as I know no economist would argue that exponential growth can go on forever – at best this is something we are uncertain about. The point is not debatable. But what conclusion can we draw from the fact that exponential growth cannot go on forever? Boulding evidently would like us to conclude that if it cannot go on forever, it cannot go on for very long. Of course that does not follow. Exponential growth might be possible for only the next ten years – or it might be possible for the next ten thousand years. If the latter, there is hardly any point in arguing over it – and a model in which exponential growth can go on forever can certainly be useful and relevant despite its obvious falsity. On the other hand if we are going to run out of resources in ten years time – then indeed fooling around with models of exponential growth is a waste of time.

The point is that philosophers' and lawyers' reasoning – trying to draw a practical conclusion from an extreme hypothetical statement – "exponential growth cannot go on forever" – is false reasoning. All the action is in the quantitative dimension: some numbers are big, some numbers are small and how big and how small matters, not whether numbers are exactly equal to zero, or "infinite."

Here is a practical application of quantitative reasoning: let's consider whether or not torture should be against the law. Notice the question is not whether or not torture is "good" or "bad" or whether it is "moral" or "immoral." A standard argument that torture should be legal is based on a simple hypothetical choice experiment. Many people if faced with a choice of torturing a suspect to determine the location of a nuclear weapon set imminently to explode in a large city would be in favor of doing so. Under those circumstances I would be prepared to do so. The conclusion is then derived that torture should be legal under these circumstances, and therefore the debate should be about when not whether torture should be legal. But in fact the conclusion does not follow.

As I indicated I would be willing to torture a suspect under the specified circumstances – yet I believe that it should be illegal for me to do so. Of course were I to be brought to trial I would hope to be let off on the grounds of necessity, or to get a Presidential pardon – but the point is that because the act is illegal – hopefully with severe penalties – I would certainly not be inclined to torture someone for frivolous reasons. Thus here is an economic argument against legalizing torture: if it is legal, despite the limited circumstances under which it is legal, then – in practice – there will be far too much torture. By the way – the evidence is overwhelming – in every instance in which a government has bureaucratized torture it has quickly gotten out of hand. But again the basic point: from an economic point of view the issue is not "will there be torture" or "will there not be torture" but "what will be the impact of making torture legal or illegal on the amount of torture that is practiced." Hypotheticals about nuclear bombs in cities do not help us answer this quantitative question.

I should also add a warning at this point. Be careful in debating lawyers and philosophers. At this point in the argument they will introduce yet another irrelevant hypothetical "suppose that torture can be made legal without leading to excessive torture – should it be legal then?" To which the only relevant answer is "don't waste my time."

If – as is likely – you aren't planning on debating any lawyers or philosophers over economic issues – at least when a behavioral economist insists that people exhibit this or that form of irrationality, please ask: how many people and how irrational is the behavior in question? Theories by their nature are false. The question is always – are they quantitatively useful or not?

## The Rush Hour Traffic Game

Beware of lawyers and philosophers bearing hypothetical examples. But beware also of social scientist bearing only laboratory results. After all – our main interest is: does the theory work outside the laboratory? In particular – does Nash equilibrium work outside the laboratory? That question is easier to answer than you might think.

There is a game that most of us are intimately familiar with. It is played five days a week in every major city in the world: it is the *rush hour traffic* game. In the "morning game" the "players" are commuters trying to get to work. Their choices are which route to take. Their objective is to minimize the time it takes to get to work – the more time it takes to get to work, the less happy you are. A moment of reflection should convince you that the sheer size of this game is overwhelming – in a large city it involves millions of players each of whom chooses between millions of routes. Yet the outcome of this game is a Nash equilibrium.

Wow! How can I possibly know that? Even the biggest supercomputer in the world can't compute the Nash equilibrium of this game. Recall, though, what a Nash equilibrium is. It simply means that each commuter is taking the quickest route given the routes of all the other commuters. So the test of the Nash equilibrium theory is a simple one: are there commuters who can find quicker routes?

This test, by the way, is why I want to focus on rush hour traffic. During non-rush times there are many inexperienced drivers on the road, some making one of a kind trips to unfamiliar locations, and often they take routes that are much slower than the fastest available. Nonetheless during rush hour commuters are experienced, and have tried a lot of routes in the past – there is no much room for learning. So – if you try to take a tricky combination of side streets rather than the main boulevard you discover that just enough traffic has spilled over on to the side streets that you can gain no advantage. How do I know this? I've tried – I suggest you do. For years I commuted about an hour to work through Los Angeles rush hour. I was often stuck on a very slow boulevard in Beverly Hills. In frustration I experimented with many alternative combinations of side streets. Sadly it never got me to work faster. In fact on one occasion, I was behind a large truck when I got off the main boulevard, and after ten minutes of tricky driving, I got back on the main boulevard – just to find myself behind exactly the same truck. In short: Nash equilibrium.

Now you may believe that I am right that what we observe at rush hour throughout the world is a Nash equilibrium. You may also wonder – since we can't possibly compute what it is – what good that observation does us. As it transpires it does us quite a bit of good – but we'll talk about that in the next chapter.

## Competitive Markets

Economists who study voting and traffic patterns are few and far between. For the most part what economists study is trade taking place in markets. And few things seem more controversial than the assertion that markets "clear." Or that markets are competitive when there are only a handful of firms. For example a former Presidential advisor, N. Gregory Mankiw writes

> New Keynesian economists, however, believe that market-clearing models cannot explain short-run economic fluctuations. (2010)

Given this controversy, the experimental evidence may surprise you: it is easy to identify what settings are competitive, and in these settings we observe exactly the price that economists expect based on theory.

The most striking example is the work by Roth et al. in 1991 examining a simple market auction with nine identical buyers. These buyers must bid on an object worth nothing to the seller, and worth $10.00 to each of them. If the seller accepts he earns the highest price offered, and a buyer selected from the winning bids by lottery earns the difference between the object's value and the bid. Each player participates in 10 different market rounds with a changing population of buyers. In all these possible situations, bids must be in increments of five cents.

What does game theory predict should happen? Suppose the highest bid is some amount, call it in the time honored tradition, $x$. If you bid $x$ then there is a tie and you have at most a 50% chance of getting the object and can earn at most an expected payoff of ($10 – $x$)/2. If you raise the bid by a nickel – you get the object with certainty – you can earn $ 9.95 – $x$. As it happens if $x$ < $ 9.90 it is better to raise by a nickel and get $ 9.95 – $x$ rather than ($10 – $x$)/2. Also if $x$ < $10 you never want to bid less than $x$ since then you would get nothing, while by bidding $x$ you would get a share of something. Finally, if everyone else bids $9.90 you can do better by bidding $9.95 getting the entire five cents for yourself, rather than a 1/9th share of ten cents. Therefore at a Nash equilibrium the winning bid has to be at least $9.95 and of course it cannot be more than $10.00.

So what happened in the laboratory? By the time the participants had played in seven auctions the price was $9.95 or $10.00 in *every* case – and in most cases this happened long before the seventh try.

Notice the key feature of this auction: no individual buyer can have much impact on the price: since everyone else is bidding $9.95 or $10.00

the question for a buyer is not so much about changing the price, but rather their willingness to buy given that price. This idea – that market participants can have little impact on prices – is a central one in the economic theory of competitive markets. The corresponding theory – the theory of *competitive equilibrium* – is an important variation on Nash equilibrium. It is a theory in which traders in markets choose their trades ignoring whatever small impact they may have on market prices. Equilibrium occurs at prices that reconcile the desire of suppliers to sell with consumers to buy.

At one time a great deal of effort was expended by economists trying to understand the mechanism by which prices adjusted. Modern economic theory recognizes that the particular way in which prices are adjusted is not so important. An important modern branch of game theory is *mechanism design* theory. While game theory takes the game as given, mechanism design theory asks – how might we design a game to achieve some desired social goal? To emphasize that the choice of the game is part of the problem, the way in which decisions of players are mapped into social outcomes is called a mechanism rather than a game.

From the mechanism design point of view, an auction is just one of many price setting mechanisms. It is a mechanism that acts to reconcile demand with supply – to clear the market. There are many mechanisms that do this. They are all equivalent in that they perform the same function of clearing markets. Consequently the exact details are of no great importance. Perhaps it is done electronically as it is the case with the Chicago Board of Trade. Or, perhaps, by shouting out orders as on the New York Stock Exchange (NYSE).

How well does the theory of competitive equilibrium and market clearing work? Let's consider a simple market with five suppliers. Suppose that each supplier faces a cost of producing output given by the following table:

| Units Produced | Cost |
|:--------------:|:----:|
| *0* | 0 |
| *20* | 905 |
| *40* | 1900 |
| *60* | 3000 |
| *240* | 17000 |

Supplier Cost

The profit of a firm is just the amount it receives from sales – its revenue – minus this cost. For any particular price we can work out from the cost data how many units should be produced to maximize profits:

| Price | Profit Maximizing Output | Corresponding Industry Output |
|:-----:|:------------------------:|:-----------------------------:|
| 100 | 240 | 1200 |
| 90 | 198 | 990 |
| 60 | 72 | 360 |
| 30 | 0 | 0 |
| 10 | 0 | 0 |

Profit Maximizing Output

I did this computation using calculus – and that is why we demand our undergraduate students know calculus. But obviously business people do not generally choose their production plans by using calculus. Rather they weigh the cost of hiring a few more workers against the additional revenue from a few more sales and decide whether or not to expand – or shrink – their operation. Of course in the end they get exactly the same result as I do by using calculus.

The price that consumers will pay depends on how many units are offered for sale in total. Suppose that this is given by the demand schedule

| Units for Sale | Sale Price |
|:--------------:|:----------:|
| 0 | 100 |
| 180 | 80 |
| 360 | 60 |
| 630 | 30 |
| 900 | 0 |

Demand Curve

Notice that for the firms to decide how much to produce they must guess what price they will face. In the competitive market clearing equilibrium – also called the rational expectations or perfect foresight equilibrium – they guess correctly. Inspecting the table for profit maximization – the supply, and the table for consumer willingness to pay – the demand, we see that when price is 60 consumers wish to purchase 360 units, and firms wish to provide this same number. Thus 60 is the price that "clears the market" or the "competitive equilibrium price."

Bear in mind that in a competitive equilibrium firms are strategically naïve. They ignore the fact that by producing less there will be less supply and consumers will be willing to pay more resulting in a higher profit. Since each firm is only 20% of the market the ability of an individual firm to manipulate prices is not large, but it is not zero either. If we apply the theory of Nash equilibrium so that each firm correctly anticipates the choices of their rival firms, then firms produce less – 63 instead of 72 – and the Nash equilibrium price is higher: 65 rather than the competitive price of 60. The difference between the Nash and competitive equilibrium is not all that great, so that even with as few as five firms, competitive equilibrium with market clearing is a reasonable approximation.

Undoubtedly, real people are not unboundedly rational. They can scarcely be expected to rationally forecast "equilibrium" prices. Let us instead consider a "behavioral" model: let us suppose that firms forecast prices next period to be whatever prices were last period. This is exactly the behavioral model of adaptive expectations formation that was widely used before the rational expectations revolution of which behavioral economists are so critical.

What happens when prices are forecast to be the same next period as last? If the starting price is 90, then firms will wish to produce 990 units of output. Consumers are not willing to buy so many units, so price falls to 0. At that price firms aren't willing to produce anything, so now price then rises to 100. The following period the industry produces 1200. The cycle then continues with the market alternating between overproduction leading to a zero price, then underproducing leading to a price of 100. This is the so-called "cobweb" although we might also refer to it as a business cycle – the failure of the capitalist system by flooding the market with cheap goods and then falling into recession. Karl Marx pointed out exactly this self-destructive tendency of capitalism.

Which theory is correct? In 2004 Sutan and Willinger implemented this market in the laboratory with real subjects playing for real money. Participants had an opportunity to play variations of this game 40 times. There were three different experimental markets. The graph below plots the actual price in each of those markets against the number of times players interact in those markets:

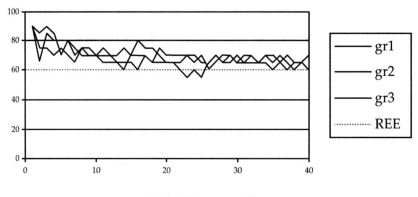

Market Prices over Time

After about the first ten periods prices fluctuate within a relatively narrow band in all three markets. It is generally higher than the rational expectations competitive price of 60, which is marked by the dotted line in the graph. Interestingly Sutan and Willinger view this as a minor contradiction of economic theory. In fact the subjects are cleverer here than the experimenters: the price is essentially the Nash equilibrium price of 65. As we shall see later it is not so uncommon for subjects to outwit experimenters. Often "anomalous" experimental results supposedly contradicting economic theory simply reflect the fact that the experimenter misunderstood what the theory says. As the fundamental theory is that of Nash equilibrium which predicts a price of 65 – the results of this experiment are just what the theory predicts. Competitive equilibrium is merely an approximation. Here it is a useful approximation as the competitive price of 60 is close to the Nash equilibrium price of 65, but it is not exact.

By way of contrast the behavioral theory does about as badly as a theory can. The average price according to the behavioral theory is 50 – much lower than the actual market price which is always above 60 – and prices remain within a tight band – they certainly do not cycle abruptly from 0 to 100.

The key point here is that while it is no doubt true that people do not have unbounded rationality, we have only very simple and naïve models of bounded rationality. It is a fact that people are very good at learning, and even very sophisticated computer programs produced over many years by very skilled computer scientists working on artificial intelligence are much less capable of learning than even small children. By contrast "behavioral" models of "bounded rationality" such as expecting next period price to equal this period price are extremely simplistic. Hence the quantitative question: is a model of unbounded rationality or an extremely primitive model of learning a better approximation to reality? In this experiment it is clear that the model of unbounded rationality is vastly better.

The results of this experiment are by no means atypical. Experiments on competitive equilibrium have been conducted many times, dating back at least to the work of Vernon Smith in 1962 – work that is hardly obscure as he won a Nobel Prize for it. Most of these experiments involve real paid subjects in the role of both buyer and seller. The results are highly robust: competitive equilibrium predicts the outcome of market experiments with a high degree of accuracy, with experimental markets converging quickly to approximately the competitive price.

# 3. Why Is the World so Irrational?

*The Al-Qassam Brigade is about killing, being killed, and the celebration of killing. None of this killing seems to serve any strategic plan, except as blind revenge, an expression of religious hysteria, and as a placeholder for a viable program for creating a Palestinian state. In short, the Al-Qassam Brigade can best be described as a psychotic death cult.* Sharkansky, 2002

One of the most frustrating experiences for a working economist is to be confronted by a psychologist, political scientist – or even in some cases Nobel Prize winning economist – to be told in no uncertain terms "Your theory does not explain X – but X happens in the real world, so your theory is wrong." The frustration revolves around the fact that the theory does predict X and you personally published a paper in a major journal showing exactly that. One cannot intelligently criticize – no matter what one's credentials – what one does not understand. We have just seen that standard mainstream economic theory explains a lot of things quite well. Before examining criticisms of the theory more closely it would be wise to invest a little time in understanding what the theory does and does not say.

The point is that the theory of "rational play" does not say what you probably think it says. At first glance, it is common to call the behavior of suicide bombers crazy or irrational – as for example in the Sharkansky quotation at the beginning of the chapter. But according to economics it is probably not. From an economic perspective suicide need not be irrational: indeed a famous unpublished 2004 paper by Nobel Prize winning economist Gary Becker and U.S. Appeals Court Judge Richard Posner called "Suicide: An Economic Approach" studies exactly when it would be rational to commit suicide.

The evidence about the rationality of suicide is persuasive. For example, in the State of Oregon, suicide is legal. It cannot, however, be legally done in an impulsive fashion: it requires two oral requests separated by at least 15 days plus a written request signed in the presence of two witnesses, at least one of whom is not related to the applicant. While the exact number of people committing suicide under these terms is not known, it is substantial. Hence – from an economic perspective – this behavior is rational because it represents a clearly expressed preference.

What does this have to do with suicide bombers? If it is rational to commit suicide, then it is surely rational to achieve a worthwhile goal in the process. Eliminating ones enemies is – from the perspective of economics – a rational goal. Moreover, modern research into suicide bombers (see Kix [2010]) shows that they exhibit exactly the same characteristics of isolation and depression that leads in many cases to suicide without bombing. That is: leaning to committing suicide they rationally choose to take their enemies with them.

# The Prisoner's Dilemma and the Fallacy of Composition

Much of the confusion about what economics does and does not say revolves around the distinction between individual self interest and what is good for society. If people are so rational how can we have war and crime and poverty and other social ills? Why do bad things happen to societies made up of rational people? The place to start understanding this non-sequiter is with the most famous of all games, the *Prisoner's Dilemma* game.

The Prisoner's Dilemma is a game so popular Google shows over 564,000 web pages devoted to it. As this game has two players it can conveniently be described by a matrix, with the choices of the first player labeling the rows, and the choices of the second player labeling the columns. Each entry in the matrix represents a possible outcome – we specify the feeling players have about that outcome by writing two numbers representing the utility or payoff to the first and second player respectively.

In the original Prisoner's Dilemma the two players are partners in a crime who at the onset of the game have been captured by the police and placed in separate cells. As is the case in every crime drama on television, each prisoner is offered the opportunity to confess to the crime. The matrix of payoffs can be written as

|  | *Not confess* | *Confess* |
|---|---|---|
| *Not confess* | 10,10 | –9,20 |
| *Confess* | 20,–9 | 2,2 |

Prisoner's Dilemma Payoffs

Each player has two possible actions – to *Confess* or to *Not confess*. The row labels represent possible choices of action by the first player "Player 1." The column labels those of the second player "Player 2." The numbers in the matrix represent *payoffs* also called *utility*. The first number applies to player 1, and the second to player 2. Higher numbers means the player likes that outcome better. Thus if player 2 chooses not to confess, then player 1 would rather confess than not, as represented by the fact that the payoff 20 is larger than the payoff 10. This reflects the fact that the police have offered him a good deal in exchange for his confession. By way of contrast, player 2 would prefer that player 1 not confess, as represented by the fact that the payoff –9 is smaller than the payoff 10. This reflects the fact that if his partner confesses but he does not, he is going to spend a substantial amount of time in prison.

We will go through the rest of the payoffs in a bit, but first – what do these numbers really mean? I want to emphasize that "utility" numbers are not meant to represent some sort of units of happiness that could be measured in the brain. Rather, economists recognize that players have preferences among the different things that can happen and are able to rank them. Assigning a utility of 10 to player 1 when the outcome is *Not Confess/Not Confess* and 20 when it is *Confess/Not Confess* is just a way of saying "Player 1 prefers the outcome *Confess/Not Confess* to the outcome *Not Confess/Not Confess*."

More broadly, if certain regularities in preferences are true – for example they satisfy *transitivity* meaning that if you prefer apples to oranges and oranges to pears, then you also prefer apples to pears – then we can find numbers that *represent* those preferences in the sense that the analyst can determine which decision the player will make by comparing the utility numbers. However, while these utility numbers exist in the brain of the analyst we do not care whether or not they exist in the brain of the person.

The meaning of the utility numbers in the Prisoner's Dilemma game is this: if neither suspect confesses, they go free, and split the proceeds of their crime which we represent by 10 units of utility for each suspect. Alternatively, if one prisoner confesses and the other does not, the prisoner who confesses testifies against the other in exchange for going free and having some other charges dismissed and prefers this to simply splitting the proceeds of the crime. We represent this with a higher level of utility: 20. The prisoner who did not confess goes to prison, represented by a low utility of –9. Similarly, if both prisoners confess, then both are given a reduced term, but both are convicted, which we represent by giving each 2 units of utility: better than not confessing when you are ratted out, but not as good as going free.

This game is fascinating for a variety of reasons. First, it is a simple representation of a variety of important strategic situations. For example, instead of *Confess/Not confess* we could label the choices "contribute to the common good" and "behave selfishly." This captures a variety of circumstances economists describe as *public goods* problems, for example the construction of a bridge. It is best for everyone if the bridge is built, but best for each individual if someone else builds the bridge. Similarly this game could describe two firms competing in the same market, and instead of *Confess/ Not confess* we could label the choices "set a high price" and "set a low price." Naturally it is best for both firms if they both set high prices, but best for each individual firm to capture the market by setting a low price while the opposition sets a high price. This is a critical feature of game theory: many apparently different circumstances – prisoners in jail; tax-payers voting on whether to build a bridge; firms competing in the market – give rise to similar strategic considerations. To understand one is to understand them all.

A second feature of the Prisoner's Dilemma game is that it is easy to find the Nash equilibrium, and it is self-evident that this is how intelligent individuals should behave. No matter what a suspect believes his partner is going to do, it is always best to confess. If the partner in the other cell is not confessing, it is possible to get 20 instead of 10. If the partner in the other cell is confessing, it is possible to get 2 instead of –9. In other words – the best course of play is to confess no matter what you think your partner is doing. This is the simplest kind of Nash equilibrium. When you confess – even not knowing whether or not your opponent is confessing – that is the best you can do. This kind of Nash equilibrium – where the best course of play does not depend on beliefs about what the other player is doing – is called a *dominant strategy equilibrium*. In a game with a dominant strategy equilibrium we expect learning to take place rapidly – perhaps even instantaneously.

The striking fact about the Prisoner's Dilemma game and the reason it exerts such fascination is that each player pursuing individually sensible behavior leads to a miserable social outcome. The Nash equilibrium results in each player getting only 2 units of utility, much less than the 10 units each that they would get if neither confessed. This highlights a conflict between the pursuit of individual goals and the common good that is at the heart of many social problems.

# Pigouvian Taxes

Now let us return to question raised in the traffic game: what good does Nash equilibrium do us if we cannot figure out what it is? The answer is straightforward: the traffic game is like the Prisoner's Dilemma. Each commuter by choosing to drive – rather than, for example, taking the bus – derives an individual advantage by getting to work faster and more conveniently. She also inflicts a cost – called by economists a *negative externality* – on everyone else by making it more difficult for them to get to work. In other words, the private value of each commuter is higher than the social value of driving. Hence, as in the Prisoner's Dilemma game, the Nash equilibrium is not for the common good: Nash equilibrium results in too many people driving – everyone would be better off if fewer people commuted by car and chose alternatives such as living closer to work, implementing car pools, or occasionally taking the bus or telecommuting.

Economists have understood the solution to this problem since Pigou's work in 1920. If we set a corrective tax – known as Pigouvian tax in honor of this French economist – and charge each commuter for the cost that they impose on others (and therefore we internalize this external cost), then Nash equilibrium will result in social efficiency. In this example social efficiency differs from the solely private interaction because of the fact that commuters do not consider the cost of congestion on other drivers. In the Prisoner's Dilemma above, by choosing to confess you cause a loss of 19 to your opponent – the external effect. If we charge a Pigouvian tax of 19 for confessing the payoffs become

|  | *Not confess* | *Confess* |
|---|---|---|
| *Not confess* | 10, 10 | –9,1 |
| *Confess* | 1,–9 | –17, –17 |

Payoffs in Prisoner's Dilemma with Pigouvian Tax

In this case the best thing to do irrespectively of your beliefs about your opponents' actions – the dominant strategy – is to *Not confess*, and everyone gets 10 instead of 2. Notice that in this example – in the resulting equilibrium – nobody actually pays the tax.

To implement a Pigouvian tax in the traffic game is not so difficult. In some circumstances it may be hard to compute the costs imposed on others. But not so in the traffic game where traffic engineers can easily do simulations to calculate the additional commuting time from each additional commuter and economists can give a relatively accurate assessment of the social cost of the lost time based on prevailing wage rates. Moreover, with modern technology, it is quite feasible to charge commuters based on congestion and location – this is done using cameras and transponders already in cities such as London.

Given that the social gain from reducing commuting time dwarfs such things as the cost of fighting a war in Afghanistan, why do not large U.S. cities charge commuters a congestion tax? Unfortunately there is another game involved – the political game. As we observed in our analysis of voting, the benefit of voting is very small when the chances of changing the outcome are small. So voters are rationally going to avoid incurring the large cost of investigating the quality of political candidates through their platforms. This is particularly the case for something like commuting – although the total benefits are large, they are spread among a very large number of people. Since voters do not spend much effort monitoring politicians, politicians have a lot of latitude in what they do – and therefore voters quite rationally distrust them.

Voters are especially suspicious of offers by politicians to raise their taxes. Those who lean left notice that a commuter tax will favor the rich – who can afford the toll – at the expense of the poor – who would be forced into public transportation. The right leaners oppose additional taxes because they are afraid the government will squander the proceeds. In the end both parties collaborate to prevent an efficient solution to the problem of congestion. The obvious compromise is to charge a commuting fee and use the revenue to reduce the local sales tax – which also disproportionately falls on the poor. However: who in the world would believe a politician's promise that this is what she will do?

Many solutions to economic problems are obvious. For example: virtually all economists favor raising the gas tax – this serves as a tax on pollution, and whatever one's views of global warming, raising the gas tax is much more desirable than mandating fuel efficiency standards for cars, which is what we currently do. Unfortunately we do not yet have a good recommendation for what to do about the problem of voters who rationally invest little in monitoring politicians and the politicians of both parties who are rationally bought and paid for by special interests. As Winston Churchill said in a speech in the House of Commons in 1947.

> No one pretends that democracy is perfect or all-wise. Indeed, it has been said that democracy is the worst form of government except all those other forms that have been tried from time to time.

## The Repeated Prisoner's Dilemma

The outcome of the Prisoner's Dilemma is counterintuitive. If a prisoner rats out his partner should he not fear future retaliation? That depends on whether he is likely to meet the partner in the future or not. Implicit in the original formulation of the problem is that the prisoners will not meet in the future. In many practical situations this is not the case.

A simple model game theorists use for studying this problem is that of the *repeated* game. Suppose that after the first game ends, and the suspects either are freed or are released from jail, they will play the same game one more time. In this case – the first time the game is played – the suspects may reason that they should not confess because if they do their partner will follow suit when the game is played again. Strictly speaking, this conclusion is not valid, since in the second game both suspects will confess no matter what happened in the first game. However, repetition opens up the possibility of being rewarded or punished in the future for current behavior, and game theorists have provided a number of theories to explain the obvious intuition that if the game is repeated often enough, the suspects ought to cooperate rather than confess.

To analyze a repeated game we must consider the fact that the utilities or payoffs are received at different time periods. As a rule payoffs you receive in the future are worth less than those you receive today – "a bird in the hand" and all that. The standard model that economists use is that of discounting the future. More formally, the *discount factor* is a positive number less than one that is used to weight payoffs received in the "next period." As an example, take the discount factor to be ¾. Suppose that 20 is received today and 12 next period. Then the *present value* consists of the 20 today plus ¾ of the 12 tomorrow, that is, 20 + 9 = 29. Notice that the discount factor depends – among other things – on the amount of time between "periods." The longer the time considered between time periods, the smaller the discount factor.

A fundamental fact about Nash equilibrium in a repeated game is that while there can be more equilibria than in the one-shot game – the game played once – there can never be fewer. That is: suppose that all players follow the strategy of playing as they would in the one-shot game no matter what their opponents do. Since it was best for each player to play that way when the game was played once, it is still best when the game is played over and over again.

There are two different kinds of repeated game: there are games that are repeated with a definite ending. For example, the game may be played once, or twice, or four times – or any finite number of times. And there are games with an indefinite ending – for example every time the game is played, say, there might be a 50% chance it will be played again and a 50% chance it will end.

In the Prisoner's Dilemma it makes quite a bit of difference whether there is a definite or indefinite ending. If there is a definite ending, then the last time the game is played everyone knows it is being played only once: thus both players confess no matter what has gone before – they not expect to interact ever again. But now think of the next to last period: everyone anticipates that no matter what happens today, tomorrow everyone will confess. Hence you might as well confess today since failing to do so will not result in favorable consideration by your partner next time around. A moment of reflection should convince you that the same is no true in the next-to-next to last period and so forth, working backwards to the first game. Consequently both players always confess.

The situation changes when there is an indefinite ending. Suppose the discount factor is $9/10$ – you can think of the discount factor as the probabilistic ending. For simplicity, limit attention to three strategies in the repeated game which we label *Grim*, *Not Confess* and *Confess*. *Not Confess* means just that: don't confess ever. Similarly *Confess* means always confess no matter what. *Grim* is trickier: don't confess the first time you play, then starting the second time the game is played do whatever the other player did the first time the game was played. If your opponent plays *Grim* like you neither player ever confesses. The same happens if your opponent plays *Not Confess*, but if he plays *Confess*, then you also confess beginning in the second period.

Let us compute the payoffs – in present value – when neither player ever confesses. In every period each player gets 10. This must be properly discounted, as a result the present value in this case is $10 + (9/10)\,10 + (9/10)^2\,10 + \dots = 100$. Here I am using the property of geometric sums that says that $\sum_{t=0}^{\infty} r^t = 1/(1-r)$ with $0 < r < 1$. More interesting is the case where a player choosing *Grim* meets an opponent playing *Confess*. The grim player gets $-9 + (9/10)\,2 + (9/10)^2\,2 + \dots = 9$ and the confessor gets $20 + (9/10)2 + (9/10)^2\,2 + \dots = 38$. The complete payoffs to all the different of combinations is shown in the matrix below:

|  | *Grim* | *Not Confess* | *Confess* |
|---|---|---|---|
| *Grim* | 100*,100* | 100,100* | 9,38 |
| *Not Confess* | 100*,100 | 100,100 | -90,200* |
| *Confess* | 38,9 | 200*,-90 | 20*,20* |

Simplified Repeated Prisoner's Dilemma Payoffs

To find the Nash equilibrium, we start by asking the hypothetical question: if your opponent played *Grim* (*Not Confess*, *Confess* respectively), what would you like to do? If you thought your opponent was playing *Grim*, you would like to either play *Grim* or to *Not Confess* as this would result in a payoff of 100 rather than 38. This is marked with an asterisk in the matrix, and is called by game theorists a *best response*. If you think your opponent is not confessing, you would like to *Confess* and get 200, and you would also like to *Confess* and get 20 if your opponent is confessing. The Nash equilibria are the mutual best responses where both players are playing best responses to each other at the same time – the cells in the matrix with two asterisks. As you can see there are two pure strategy Nash equilibria – we leave the third Nash equilibrium using randomization for later analysis. As we observed – the original Nash equilibrium of the one-shot game at *Confess-Confess* is still a Nash equilibrium. Further there is an additional Nash equilibrium: *Grim-Grim*. If your opponent is playing *Grim* you do not want to cross her by confessing – the gain of 20 for one period is more than offset by the fact that you will lose 8 every period forever after.

Does that sound a bit theoretical? In 2005 Pedro Dal Bo took the Prisoner's dilemma theory to the laboratory. He had players play the one-shot game. He had them play for two periods and for four periods (without any discounting). And then he had them play an indefinite ending – he had them play "dice games" where at the end of each round a dice was used to determine whether play would continue. He studied games where the chance of continuing was ½ and also games where it was ¾. To give players a chance to "learn their way to equilibrium" each player played 10 of these repeated games. The table below reports how often players succeeded in cooperating (not confessing) based on the type of game and how experienced players were.

| *Percentage of Cooperation* | | *Experience* | | |
|---|---|---|---|---|
| | | 1 | 2–6 | 7–10 |
| *Dice* | $\frac{1}{2}$ | 28% | 28% | 36% |
| | $\frac{3}{4}$ | 40% | 34% | 46% |
| *One Shot* | | 26% | 14% | 6.4% |
| *Finite* | 2 | 20% | 13% | 8.9% |
| | 4 | 32% | 27% | 18% |

Percentage of Cooperation

Recall the predictions of the theory. In the one-shot and finite games players should not cooperate. Inexperienced players do cooperate in violation of the theory. This had also been remarked on by earlier investigators who concluded the theory was deficient. However, as players become more experienced their willingness to cooperate declines dramatically. Even when the game is repeated four times, cooperation falls to 18%, less than is the case in any game with inexperienced players. By way of contrast, in the dice games there are equilibria where players do not cooperate, but also equilibria in which they do. Here – in comparison to the finite length games – cooperation rather than diminishing over time actually increases over time. When there is a ¾ chance the game will continue – meaning on average the game will last four periods – experienced players cooperate 46% of the time.

## Altruism and the Prisoner's Dilemma

The theory of Nash equilibrium does not perfectly describe how people played in Dal Bo's experiment. Some cooperation is taking place with relatively experienced players even when the game has a definite ending. This is not completely unexpected as in laboratory experiments about 10–20% of the participants are not paying attention to the instructions and play in a way unpredictable by any theory, rational or behavioral. The presence of a modest number of foolish players is a topic we will take up later. For the moment notice that the 18% of experienced cooperators during four period games cannot easily be dismissed as "inattentive."

What conclusion can we reach about these "irrational" cooperators? One possibility is that they engage in a kind of magical reasoning that "if I cooperate then my opponent will cooperate," or "the only way we can beat this dilemma is if we both cooperate so I better cooperate." However, unless players are mind readers, this reasoning is wrong: there can be no causal link between what you do in the privacy of your own computer booth, and your unknown opponent does in hers. Experienced players have had ample opportunity to learn the fallacy of this reasoning, so it is difficult to explain their play this way.

A more likely explanation is players are rational and *altruistic* in the technical sense that they care not only about their own monetary payoff, but also that of their opponent. It is, after all, our common experience that some people are sometimes altruistic and as we shall see, we observe altruism in many other laboratory experiments.

A second possibility is that players have not completely learned the equilibrium. That is, if players start out cooperating in hopes of eliciting future cooperation, the first thing they will discover is that it is a mistake to cooperate in the fourth period. After players stop cooperating in the fourth period they will then discover it is a mistake to cooperate in the third period – and it may take a while before they stop cooperating in the first period. The fact that this can take a long while was first shown in simulations by John Nachbar in 1989.

What can we say about these two explanations? Economists have studied altruism for many years – it was central to Barro's 1984 study of who bears the burden of taxes, for example. Yet while it is certainly real it is often ignored by economists because it is quantitatively small. People do give to charities, but for example in the United States – which has the highest rate of giving – only about 2.2–2.3% of Gross Domestic Product (GDP) is given. Moreover some of this is not strictly speaking "charitable" but rather fee for services, such as the 35% of donations that are given to religious organizations (GivingUSA, 2009). Further, as we shall see, in experiments where we can measure the relative contribution of "behavioral" preferences such as altruism and imperfect learning, imperfect learning is two to three times more important.

Despite the fact that it is unimportant in many settings, a little bit of altruism can go a long way – for example, a willingness to be altruistic only in the final period of a repeated game can dramatically change the strategic nature of the game. A player who is willing to cooperate in the final period can hold that out as a prospective reward to a not so altruistic opponent, and so get them to cooperate. This sort of altruism – kind to those people who are kind to you – is called *reciprocal altruism*. It is present in Dal Bo's experiment. From his data we can look at the final period of the two period games with a definite ending. Against an experienced player (one who has already engaged in six or more matches) if you cheat in the first period probability of getting cooperation in the final period is only 3.2% – much less than the 6.4% chance of finding an experienced cooperative opponent in the one-shot game. On the other hand, if you cooperate the chance of getting cooperation in the final round jumps to 21% - much higher than the 6.4% cooperation in the one-shot case.

Reciprocal cooperation is interesting and much studied for two reasons: first, because in games taking place over time it has a big impact on equilibrium outcomes. Second, because it is difficult to distinguish from strategic non-altruistic behavior. That is: did I take care of my aged parent because I am altruistic or because I want to get an inheritance? Even in the experimental laboratory we must worry that the students who are the experimental subjects get together and share experiences afterwards. If I am a poor liar, I may be reluctant to behave selfishly in fear that I may spill the beans to my friends, and so earn their disrespect – a fate fare worse than losing a few dollars in the laboratory.

Although altruism has been studied by economists for many years, the *social preferences* of fairness and reciprocal altruism have not been as thoroughly examined, and are a major subject of current research interest by economists such as Rabin [1993], Levine [1998], Fehr and Schmidt [1999], Bolton and Ockenfels [2000], Gul and Pesendorfer [2004], and Cox, Friedman and Sadiraj [2008].

## Do Better People Make a Better Society?

We can demonstrate some of the power and meaning of game theory by considering the following statement: "If we were all better people the world would be a better place." This may seem to be self-evidently true.

Or you may recognize that as a matter of logic this involves the fallacy of composition: just because a statement applies to each individual person it need not apply to the group. Game theory can give precise meaning to the statement of both what it means to be better people and what it means for the world to be a better place, and so makes it possible to prove or disprove the statement.

A sensible meaning of "being a better person" is to obey the biblical injunction to "love your neighbor as yourself" – that is, to be altruistic. If I truly value you – my neighbor – as myself, then I should place the same value on your utility as on my own: simply adding the two together. Hence if my selfish utility is 20 and yours is –9, my "altruistic utility" is just the sum of the two, that is to say, 11. If we begin with the payoffs in the Prisoner's Dilemma game above, we may proceed in this way to compute the payoffs in the *Biblical Game*:

|  | *Not confess* | *Confess* |
|---|---|---|
| *Not confess* | 20*,20* | 11*,11 |
| *Confess* | 11,11* | 4,4 |

Biblical Game Payoffs

This game is easy to analyze: it has a dominant strategy equilibrium. No matter what you do and what I think you will do, the best thing for me to do is not to confess. For that reason the Nash equilibrium is that neither of us confesses and consequently we both get 10 – clearly a better outcome than the original equilibrium outcome of the Prisoner's Dilemma game where we each get 2. As a result it seems if we were perfect people the world would be a better place.

The assertion, however, was not "if we were all perfect people the world would be a better place," but rather "if we were all better people the world would be a better place." A simple example adapted from Martin Osborne's [2003] textbook illustrates the basic concept. Consider the *Bus Seating Game*. There is only one vacant bench on a bus and two passengers. If both passengers sit on the bench, both receive 2. If both stand, both receive 1 as it is less pleasant to stand than to sit. If one sits and one stands, the sitting passenger gets 3 as it is more pleasant to sit by one's self than to share a bench, and the standing passenger gets 0 as it is more pleasant to share the discomfort of standing than to watch someone else seated in comfort. The payoff matrix of this game is given below:

|  | *Sit* | *Stand* |
|---|---|---|
| *Sit* | 2*,2* | 3*,0 |
| *Stand* | 0,3* | 1,1 |

Bus Seating Game Payoffs

Here it is a dominant strategy for each passenger to sit and the dominant strategy equilibrium is *Sit/Sit*. Moreover, this is a desirable outcome – *Pareto efficient* in the sense that it cannot be improved on for both players – in that both players get 2 rather than one. In other words, by making one player better off we will be making the other player worse off.

Next suppose that rather than love our neighbor as ourselves, we are excessively altruistic, caring only about the comfort of our fellow passengers. In this *Polite Bus Seating Game* the payoffs are:

|  | *Sit* | *Stand* |
|---|---|---|
| *Sit* | 2,2 | 0,3* |
| *Stand* | 3*,0 | 1*,1* |

Polite Bus Seating Game Payoffs

In this game it is dominant for both passengers to stand – that is the Nash equilibrium is *Stand/Stand* – and both get 1 rather than 2. By excessive altruism, a game with a socially good dominant strategy equilibrium – *Sit/Sit* – is converted into a Prisoner's Dilemma type of situation with a socially bad dominant strategy equilibrium.

Now you may feel this is unfair: perhaps excessive politeness and caring only about other people and not ourselves is perhaps not what we mean by "being a better person" and certainly is not very realistic. But the central idea – that the changes in payoffs due to greater altruism can change incentives in such a way so as to lead to a less favorable equilibrium is true more broadly. If we consider situations in which players have more than two strategies, we can cause a switch to a less favorable equilibrium with a more sensible and moderate interpretation of what it means to be a "better person." The game we will use to illustrate this is a variant on the repeated

Prisoner's Dilemma game with discount factor $9/10$ that we studied earlier. There we considered three strategies: *Not Confess* ever, always *Confess* and *Grim*. In this game, instead of *Grim*, there is a strategy called *Tough*. This is similar to *Grim*, except that if you play *Tough* you get a bonus of 15 at a cost to your opponent of 35. Hence the *Tough Game* has payoff matrix given by:

|  | *Tough* | *Not confess* | *Confess* |
|---|---|---|---|
| *Tough* | 80*,80* | 115,65 | 24*,3 |
| *Not confess* | 65,115 | 100,100 | -90,200* |
| *Confess* | 3,24* | 200*,-90 | 20,20 |

Tough Game Payoffs

Using the tool of best-responses, we see that this game has a unique Nash equilibrium of *Tough-Tough* giving both players 80. We can easily show this is the only possible equilibrium using a method called *iterated dominance*. Notice that *Not confess* is dominated by *Tough,* since no matter what the other player is doing, *Tough* always does better. Hence we throw out the strategy of *Not confess* and get a smaller game presented below:

|  | *Tough* | *Confess* |
|---|---|---|
| *Tough* | 80,80 | 24,3 |
| *Confess* | 3,24 | 20,20 |

Reduced Tough Game Payoffs

In this reduced game, we see that *Tough-Tough* is a dominant strategy equilibrium: this procedure of eliminating dominated strategies is called iterated dominance, and experimental evidence suggests that players learn their way to equilibrium without much difficulty in such games.

The Tough Game is very different than the Prisoner's Dilemma game: while the unique equilibrium is not quite the best possible – players get 80 rather than the 100 they would get if the both played *Not confess* it is still quite a bit better than the 20 they each get from *Confessing*. In this sense the Tough Game is very like the Bus Seating Game in that the equilibrium is rather good for both players.

What happens if we "become better people?" Let us now take the reasonable interpretation that while I care about you, I am not completely altruistic. Suppose in particular that I place a weight of two on my selfish utility and a weight of one on yours. So, for example, in the Tough Game, if I get 65 and you get 15 then in the *Altruistic Tough Game* I get 2 × 65 + 115 = 245. The payoffs in the Altruistic Tough Game can be computed as:

|             | *Tough*   | *Not Confess* | *Confess* |
|-------------|-----------|---------------|-----------|
| *Tough*       | 240,240   | 295,245*      | 51,30     |
| *Not Confess* | 245*,295  | 300,300       | −20,310*  |
| *Confess*     | 30,51     | 310*,−20      | 60*,60*   |

Altruistic Tough Game Payoffs

What happens? Using the tool of the best-response – look at those cells in the matrix with two asterisks – we see that the only equilibrium is the one in which both player *Confess*. When we compare the Tough Game to the Altruistic Tough Game, we see that greater altruism has disrupted the *Tough-Tough* equilibrium by causing players to generously switch to *Not confess* in order to give 55 to their opponent at a cost of only 5 to themselves. Unfortunately this does not result in an equilibrium: when both players are *Not confessing* they are still selfish enough to prefer to *Confess*.

Our conclusion? Far from making us better off, when we both become more altruist and more caring about one another, instead of us both getting a relatively high utility each period of 8, the equilibrium is disrupted, and we wind up in a situation in which we both get a utility each period of only 2. Notice how we can give a precise meaning to the "world being a better place." If we both receive a utility of 2 per period rather than both receiving a utility of 8 per period, we agree the world is a worse place regardless of how altruistic or selfish we happen to be – or even how concerned about fairness we might be.

The key to game theory and to understanding why better people may make the world a worse place is to understand the delicate balance of equilibrium. It is true that if we simply become more caring and nothing else happens the world will at least be no worse. However: if we become more caring we will wish to *change* how we behave. In this example in which we both try to do this at the same time, the end result will make us all worse off.

We can put this in the context of day-to-day life: if we were all more altruistic we would choose to forgive and forget more criminal behavior – to turn the other cheek. The behavior of criminals has a complication though.

More altruistic criminals would choose to commit fewer crimes. However, as crime is not punished so severely, they would be inclined to commit more crimes. If in the balance more crimes are committed, the world could certainly be a worse place. Our example shows how this might work.

The example of the Tough Game is very simple and not especially realistic. It is based on a 2008 academic paper by Hwang and Bowles. If you know some basic calculus the paper is very readable. They provide a much more persuasive and robust example tightly linked to experimental evidence showing how altruism can hurt cooperation.

## Is Compromise Good?

The Tough Game illustrates a situation where the extremes are better than the intermediate case. If people are completely selfish the world is reasonably good; if they are completely altruistic it is even better, but if they are neither completely selfish nor completely altruistic then the world is a miserable place. Situations where a compromise is worse than either extreme are not so uncommon in economic analysis. Two important practical examples are the cases of bank regulation and of health insurance.

In the case of bank regulation, we have a system where deposits are insured by the Federal Government, which also oversees bank portfolios to ensure that banks do not engage in overly risky behavior. Some economists argue that a system without regulation and insurance would be a superior system. Others think the regulatory regime is better. Yet all economists agree that a system in which deposits are guaranteed – either explicitly through an insurance agency such as the FDIC or implicitly through "too big to fail" – and bank portfolios are not regulated would be a disaster. Then banks would acquire portfolios that promised a high rate of return but also a high risk of getting wiped out. Depositors and issuers of short-term bonds would head for the banks that offered the highest returns – knowing that the U.S. Treasury and Federal Reserve System will bail them out if things go south. Which of course eventually they will – leaving the taxpayer holding the bag. Does that sound familiar? It has happened twice in the last quarter century – during the Savings and Loan crisis of the late 1980s, and again in the crisis of 2008. Beware when bankers or other crony capitalists appear before Congress or State Legislatures arguing the merits of "deregulation." What they mean is that they should be allowed to do whatever they want – especially paying themselves huge salaries for doing it – but that when things go wrong taxpayers should pay for all the losses.

Economists are not perfect people – like anyone else we put more weight on our own selfish interest than the common good. Because of this I am sure that some economists have managed to argue that this kind of "partial deregulation" is a good idea. However no economist who is not being paid to do so would argue for such a policy, and even those who do know better.

A similar problem arises with respect to health insurance. It is popular to argue that insurance companies should not be allowed to discriminate based on whether people are sick. After all, what good is insurance that you can't have when you need it? However: if the decision to participate in health insurance is voluntary, then in such a system nobody would buy insurance until they were sick – meaning that there would be no health insurance at all. Economists refer to this as "adverse selection" – only the bad risks choose to get insured. Therefore we can have a system that excludes people based on pre-existing conditions, and we can have a system that does not discriminate but in which coverage is mandatory. Certainly the system that is halfway in between does not work. The reason that employer based health insurance works is because coverage is mandatory – if you work for that employer you must accept their health insurance. Indeed, as health care costs rise eventually only sick people will choose to work for firms that offer health insurance, while the healthy will choose to earn a substantially higher wage working for a firm that does not offer insurance. When that happens, the employer-based system will break down.

## Bank Runs and the Crisis

The financial market meltdown in October 2009 has convinced many that markets are irrational, and rational models are doomed to failure. Only behavioral models recognizing the emotional "animal spirits" of investors can hope to capture the events that occur during a full blown financial panic. Most of this sentiment springs, however, from confusion about what rationality is and what rational models say.

Is it irrational to run for the exit when someone screams that the movie theater is on fire? Let's analyze this problem using the tools of rational game theory. There are effectively two options: to exit in an orderly fashion, or to rush for the exit. To keep things simple, we'll put your choice on the vertical and what everyone else does on the horizontal in the payoff matrix of this game. If everyone else is orderly and you rush, you get to the exit first, so are sure of escaping the fire. Let's give this 10 units of utility. If you exit in an orderly way, you may not be first, consequently there is a chance – say 10% – you will be caught in the fire. Let's assign that event a utility of 9. If everyone rushes and you are orderly, then you are likely not to escape – let's assign that a utility of 0. If you rush along with everyone else, then you have a chance of escape – but less than if everyone exits in an orderly way, so let's say that has a utility of 5. The table below shows your payoffs in this game:

|  | *Everyone else* | |
|---|---|---|
| *You* | Orderly | Rush |
| *Orderly* | 9 | 0 |
| *Rush* | 10 | 5 |

Fire in the Theater Payoffs

This is simply a variation of the Prisoner's Dilemma game. No matter what you think everyone else is doing – the dominant strategy for you is to rush. Of course in the resulting equilibrium everyone gets 5, while if they all exited in an orderly way they would all get 9.

Notice that the theory of rational play has no problem explaining the fact that everyone rushes for the exits – indeed that is exactly what the theory predicts. Nowhere do we model the very real sick feeling of panic that people feel as they rush for the exits. That is a symptom of being in a difficult situation, not an explanation of why people behave as they do. It isn't paranoia if they are really out to get you.

The situation in a market panic is similar. Suppose you turn on the television and notice the Chairman of the Federal Reserve Board, hands trembling slightly, giving a speech indicating that the financial sector is close to meltdown. It occurs to you that when this happens, stocks will not have much value. Naturally you wish to sell your stocks – and to do so before they fall in price, which is to say, to sell before everyone else can rush to sell. Thus there is a "panic" as everyone rushes to sell. Individual behavior here is rational – and unlike the rushing to the exits where more lives would be spared if the exodus was orderly, in the stock market there is no real harm if people rush to sell rather than selling in an orderly way.

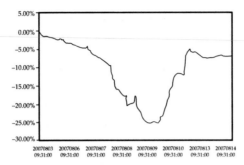

Panel (a): Minute by-Minute Data from the Quant Event 2007

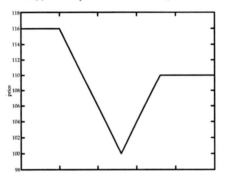

Panel (b): Theoretically Predicted Price Path

In some circumstances people overdo it – and the price drops so much that it bounces right back up as soon as people get their wits back. Perhaps this is due to irrationality? Not at all – there is a beautiful paper written in 2009 by Lasse Pedersen analyzing the so-called "quant event" of August 3–14 2007, where prices did exactly that. The first figure above shows the minute by minute real market price and the second figure shows prices computed from the theory. The two figures speak for themselves. The key thing to understand is that the theory is of pure rational expectations – irrationality, psychology, and "behavioral" economics do not enter the picture.

The same idea applies to bank runs. If you think your bank is going to fail taking your life savings with it, it is perfectly rational to try to get your money out as quickly as you can. If everyone does that it pretty much guarantees the bank will fail. A formal model of bank runs along these lines was first proposed by Diamond and Dybvig in the prestigious *Journal of Political Economy* in 1983. And no, I'm not picking some obscure paper that nobody in economics has paid any attention to – according to Google there have been 3,639 follow up papers. So far nobody has pointed out any facts or details about the financial crisis that is inconsistent with or fails to be predicted by these models of rational behavior.

# Rational Expectations and Crashes

One problem with defending economics in public forums is that people you don't know write you emails. The most common theme is "You guys didn't predict the crisis so you are useless." I'm not entirely clear on why the only possible use of economics should be to predict crises, but I can at least sympathize with the idea that failing to predict a giant crisis is a huge failure.

But is it? Step back a moment. Suppose that we could. We'd run a big computer program that all economists agreed was right, and everyone else believed, and it would tell us "Next week the stock market will fall 20%." What would you do? Knowing the stock market will drop 20% next week, would you wait until next week to sell? Of course not, you'd want to dump your stocks before everyone else did. And when everyone tried to do that the stock market would drop by 20% – but not next week, it would happen right now. You don't wait until you feel the flames before you rush for the theater exits.

Put another way, there is an intrinsic interaction between the forecaster and the forecast – at least if the forecaster is believed. Predicting economic activity isn't like predicting the weather. Whether or not there is going to be a hurricane doesn't depend on whether or not we *think* there is going to be a hurricane. Whether or not there is going to be an economic crisis depends on whether or not we think there is going to be one. And this is why the economics profession came to adopt the rational expectations model. Unlike behavioral models – which treat economic activity like hurricanes – the rational expectations model captures the intrinsic connection between the forecaster and the forecast. In fact one description of a model of rational expectations is that it describes a world where the forecaster has no advantage in making forecasts over anyone else in the economy – which if people believe his forecasts will have to be the case.

Did you get that? When people speak of "self-fulfilling prophecies" they aren't talking about models of irrational behavior. Models of irrational behavior do not predict that there can be "self-fulfilling prophecies." Only models of rational behavior do.

Let's look at the criticism of the economics profession for having failed to predict the crisis more closely. One articulate critic of modern economics is a Nobel Prize winning economist – a New York Times columnist by the name of Paul Krugman who wrote in 2009 about

> ...the profession's blindness to the very possibility of catastrophic failures in a market economy. During the golden years, financial economists came to believe that markets were inherently stable – indeed, that stocks and other assets were always priced just right. There was nothing in the prevailing models suggesting the possibility of the kind of collapse that happened last year.

But is that true? Some years earlier, in 1979, an economist wrote a paper called "A Model of Balance-of-Payments" showing how under perfect foresight crises are ubiquitous when speculators swoop in and sell short. The paper is deficient in that it supposes that crises are perfectly foreseen and – as indicated above – this cannot lead to catastrophic drops in prices. However, the paper is not obscure, there having been some 2,354 follow-on papers, including a beautiful paper written in 1983 by Steve Salant. Salant uses the tools of modern economics, in which the fundamental forces driving the economy are not perfectly foreseen, to show how rational expectations lead to speculation and unexpected yet catastrophic price drops. Lest you think that this 27 year old paper is lost in the mists of time... in 2001 I published a paper with Michele Boldrin entitled "Growth Cycles and Market Crashes." The message was most assuredly not that the "kind of collapse that happened last year" is impossible or even unlikely.

Despite the fact that the idea of the Salant paper is integral to most modern economic models, it still never fails to surprise non-economists when market crises do occur. It has happened in England, Mexico, Argentina, Israel, Italy, Indonesia, Malaysia, Russia, and of course more than once in the United States. Perhaps policy makers and ordinary citizens should pay more attention to economists? The plaintiveness and whining when it happens are always the same: for example, in 1992, nine years after the Salant paper, Erik Ipsen reported in the *New York Times* that

> Sweden's abandonment Thursday of its battle to defend the krona, in a grudging capitulation to currency speculators, bodes ill for Europe's other weak currencies and threatens to send new waves of turbulence through the European Monetary System.
>
> The central bank, which jacked interest rates to an astronomical 500 percent to stave off devaluation during the European currency crisis in September, raised rates to 20 percent Thursday morning, from 11.5 percent, in a last attempt to bolster the krona, only to concede defeat hours later.
>
> "The speculative forces just proved too strong," Prime Minister Carl Bildt said in announcing that Sweden would let the krona float.

Those who forget history are doomed to repeat it. Oh, by the way – the author of that 1979 paper pointing out the ubiquity of crises? Paul Krugman.

# The Economic Consequences of John Maynard Keynes

We have got quite a bit of mileage from variations of the theme of running for the exits – from the Prisoner's dilemma game. But this is not the only game fraught with economic consequence. The *coordination game* – introduced by Thomas Schelling in 1960 – is another simple model with significant ramifications.

In the story told by Schelling, two strangers are told to meet in New York City on a specific day, but are unable to communicate with each other about the meeting place. Bear in mind that Schelling was writing in 1960, when the modern cell phone was not even a gleam in the science fiction novelists' eye. It turns out that most people manage to say "noon in Grand Central station," meaning that they mostly succeed in meeting each other.

To analyze this game theoretically, let's imagine that the only other possible meeting place is Times Square. Specifically, we'll suppose that the game matrix is a slight variation on the game analyzed by Schelling:

|  | *Grand Central* | *Times Square* |
|---|---|---|
| *Grand Central* | 3*,3* | 0,0 |
| *Times Square* | 0,0 | 2*,2* |

Schelling's Meeting Game Payoffs

Here if they miss connections they get nothing, but we assume that since Times Square is more crowded than Grand Central, that they get slightly less – two instead of three – if they try to meet there.

This game is very different than the prisoner's dilemma in that the interests of the two players are perfectly aligned – I would like to coordinate with you to meet at the same place. In particular, altruism or "goodness" has no role to play in this game. You might think that is pretty much the end of the story, but analysis of Nash equilibrium shows it is not. If you think the other person is going to Times Square – you should do the same. As a result the game has two rather than one pure-strategy Nash equilibrium, one where they meet at Grand Central and one where they meet in Times Square. There is also a Nash equilibrium involving randomization – I will talk about this later.

"This is silly," you say, obviously Grand Central is better, we'll meet there. And economists and game theorist agree. Alternatively suppose that it is much worse to be in Grand Central by yourself than in Times Square, so that the payoffs are really.

|  | *Grand Central* | *Times Square* |
| --- | --- | --- |
| *Grand Central* | 3*,3* | –10,0 |
| *Times Square* | 0,–10 | 2*,2* |

Grand Central Meeting Game Payoffs

Now are you so sure it is a good idea to go to Grand Central? After all if you are wrong about the other person you'll be stuck with –10, while if you go to Times Square and the other person doesn't show up you at least get 0. Similarly the other person reasoning the same way may also head to Times Square.... Then, in fact the relevant Nash equilibrium of this game may be *Times Square/Times Square*. This is worse than meeting in Grand Central – both get 2 instead of 3, and it is called a *coordination failure equilibrium*.

There is a theory of these coordination failure equilibria – but the concept of risk dominance that is used to analyze it and the probabilistic theory of learning that was created by Kandori, Mailath and Rob, and by Peyton Young in 1993 is too mathematical and complex to describe here. However – if you are a fan of the idea that economics spends too much time on rationality and not enough time on evolution, let me point out that these famous and highly cited articles employ…an evolutionary model.

That is digressive. The key point is that insofar as anybody has been able to make head or tails out of the confusing jumble of thought found in John Maynard Keyes *General Theory of Employment, Interest and Money*, it is the idea that there can be a coordination failure. That is, firms don't produce because they don't think anybody will buy their products, and consumers don't buy because they don't have any money because firms won't employ them. There is no doubt that this makes logical sense – enough so that current pundits such as the ubiquitous Professor Krugman still wish to convince us that Keynes makes sense. The fact that nobody has been able to make sense out of Keynes isn't because of ill-will or lack of effort on the part of the economics profession, however. Google shows some of the articles I've discussed with as many as several thousand citations; Keynes book, on the other hand, garners over ten thousand – and those are only the citations available by computer, which, since the book was published in 1936, misses most of them.

No, the problem with Keynes isn't that it is impossible to construct a plausible yet logical model of what he had in mind. It's just that every attempt to construct such a model has fallen victim of the evidence. First of all, if coordination failure was that easy, we would see it all the time – yet we've only had one Great Depression. At the time of the Great Depression, of course, models of the ubiquity of great depressions were very popular. For example, the leading growth model at that time was the Harrod-Domar model that said that the capitalist economy teetered on the razor's edge, ready to fall into depression at an instant notice. It is perhaps unfortunate that the model was created between 1939 and 1946 – immediately proceeding one of the longest unbroken spells of growth and prosperity in history.

There have been valiant attempts – for example Leijonhufvud's 1973 notion that there is a "classical corridor" in which as long as only moderately bad things happen, the economy behaves classically as predicted by some of the very early rational expectations models. However if something big and bad enough occurs – the collapse of the housing market? – then we are thrust into a Keynesian world of coordination failure.

The key problem is that Keynesian models are extremely delicate – writing in 1992 Jones and Manuelli show that coordination failure can occur only under very implausible assumptions about the economy. More to the point – there simply isn't any empirical evidence pointing to coordination failure. We are rebounding from the current crisis – the theory of Keynes says we should not be doing so. Additionally modern analysis of the Great Depression, such as that of Cole and Ohanian [2004] suggests that the prolonged length of the depression was due more to bad government policies – the crony capitalism of the New Deal, for example – than to an intrinsic inability of a capitalist economy to right itself.

# 4. Does Economic Theory Fail?

Economic theory works some of the time. But perhaps not always? There is an experimental literature that argues there are gross violations of economic theory. Since these failures are not with the theory of Nash equilibrium, I will explain an important variation – the notion of subgame perfect equilibrium. How well does the theory of subgame perfection do in the laboratory? In three games – a public goods game called Best-shot, a bargaining game called Ultimatum and the game of Grab-a-dollar the simple theory with selfish players fails.

## Subgame Perfection

Our notion of a game is a matrix game in which players simultaneously choose actions one time and one time only. Situations like this are rare outside the laboratory. The "real" theory of games has long-since incorporated both the presence of time – and that ubiquitous phenomenon known as uncertainty. Often when I am teaching a course and I get to this point, I say "now we start the real theory of games." So let us begin.

A "real" game involves players taking moves. Some may be simultaneous, in other cases we get to make choices after observing what other people have done. For example, we generally buy groceries after the store has posted the prices. To keep things easy, focus on sequential move games – although the complete theory allows both simultaneous and sequential moves. We model sequential moves by a *game tree*, a diagram of circles and arrows, with the circles indicating that a player is making a move, and the arrows the options available to that player. Below is illustrated a simple and famous example, the *Selten Game*:

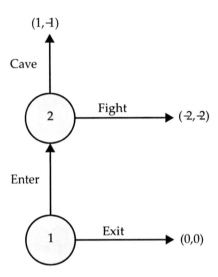

Selten Game Tree

In this simple game player 1 moves first. Her *decision node* is represented by the circle labeled with her name "1." She has two choices represented by arrows: to *Enter* the market or *Exit* the market. If she *exits*, the game ends and everyone gets a payoff of zero. If she *enters*, player 2 gets to move, as represented by the circle labeled with "2." Player 2 has two possible responses to entry: either to *Fight*, or to *Cave*. If he fights, everyone loses, as indicated by the numbers ⟨2, ⟨2 representing the payoff to player 1 and player 2 respectively. If he Caves, player 1 wins and gets 1, while player 2 loses and gets ⟨1. Notice that for player 2 it is better to *cave* and avoid the *fight*. Note the sequential nature of this game – player 2 gets to play only if player 1 decides to *enter*.

There are two ways to play this game. One is to play it as described. The other is to make advance plans. The idea of advance plans, or *strategies* is the heart of game theory. A strategy is a set of instructions that you can give to a friend – or program on a computer – explaining how you would like to play the game. It is a complete set of instructions: it must explain how to play in every circumstance that can arise in the game. As you can imagine this may not be very practical: think of trying to write down instructions for a friend to play a chess game on your behalf. Chess has a myriad of possible configurations – and you have to tell your friend how to play in each possible situation. Of course the IBM Corporation did provide a very effective set of instructions to the computer Deep Blue – so effective that Deep Blue beat the human world chess champion in 1997. For the rest of us implementing complex and effective strategies may not be so practical, but regardless, the idea of a strategy is very useful conceptually.

In the Selten Game, each player has two strategies. Player 1 can either *exit* or *enter*, and player 2 can either *fight* or *cave*. Notice that player 2's strategy is conceptually different from player 1's. Player 1's strategy is a definite decision to do something. Player 2's strategy is hypothetical: "if I get to play the game, here is what I will do."

Strategies are chosen in advance – and each player has to choose a strategy without knowing what the other player has chosen. Thus, when the game is described by means of strategies it is a matrix game: each player chooses a strategy, and depending on the strategies chosen, they get payoffs. The matrix that goes with the Selten Game is below:

|  | *Fight* | *Cave* |
|---|---|---|
| *Enter* | -2,-2 | 1*,-1* (SGP) |
| *Exit* | 0*,0*(Nash) | 0,0* |

Selten Game Payoffs

Notice how when player 1 chooses to *exit* it doesn't matter what player 2 does – in that case player 2 does not get the chance to play.

We can analyze this game using our usual tools of best-response and Nash equilibrium. As marked in the matrix: if player 2 is going to *fight*, it is best for player 1 to *exit*; if player 2 is going to *cave* it is best for player 1 to *enter*. If player 1 is going to *enter*, it is best for player 2 to *cave*. If player 1 is going to *exit*, players do not interact at all, so it doesn't really matter what player 2 does: she is *indifferent*.

The game has two Nash equilibria – *exit/fight* labeled "Nash" and *enter/ cave* labeled "SGP" for reasons to be explained momentarily. Here is the thing: *exit/fight* while a Nash equilibrium is not completely plausible. Player 1 may reason to herself – if I were to *enter* rather than *exit*, it would not be in player 2's interest to *fight*. So I believe that if I *enter* he will *cave*. In conclusion I see that I should go ahead and *enter*.

The notion that player 1 should enter is captured by the notion of *subgame perfect equilibrium*. This insists that not only should the strategies form an equilibrium, but, since (or if!) we believe the theory of Nash equilibrium, in every subgame the strategies in that subgame should also form a Nash equilibrium. In the Selten Game, there is one subgame: the game in which player 1 had chosen to *enter* – the subgame is very simple, it just consists of player 2 choosing whether to *fight* or to *cave*. It can be represented in matrix form as

| *Fight* | *Cave* |
|:---:|:---:|
| -2,-2 | 1,-1 |

Selten Subgame Payoffs

As there is only one player in this subgame, the Nash equilibrium is obvious -1 is better than -2 so player 2 should *cave*.

This analysis is fine as far as it goes. But if I were player 2 and was discussing the game with player 1 before we played I would say "Don't you dare enter – if you do I will fight." I would say this because if I could convince player 1 of my willingness to fight he wouldn't enter, and I would get 0 instead of □1. In game theory this is called *commitment* or *precommitment*, and is of enormous importance.

A practical example of the Selten game is the game played by the United States and Soviet Union during the Cold War – with nuclear weapons. We may imagine that player 1 is the Soviet Union, and *entry* corresponds to "invade Western Europe," while *fight* means that the United States will respond with strategic nuclear weapons – effectively destroying the entire world. Naturally if the Soviet Union were to take over Western Europe it would hardly be rational for the United States to destroy the world. On the other hand, by persuading the Soviet Union of our irrational willingness to do this, we prevented them (perhaps) from invading Western Europe. As Richard Nixon instructed Henry Kissinger to say to the Russians "I am sorry, Mr. Ambassador, but [the president] is out of control... you know Nixon is obsessed about Communism. We can't restrain him when he is angry – and he has his hand on the nuclear button."

From a game-theoretic point of view, the game with commitment is a different game than the game without. In the *Stackelberg Game* illustrated below player 2 moves first and chooses whether to *play* or *commit*. If he chooses to *play* then the original game is played. If he chooses to *commit*, then a different game is played with the same structure and in which one payoff has been changed: the payoff to *cave* which is now -3 rather than -1. That is, the role of the commitment is to make it more expensive to *cave*.

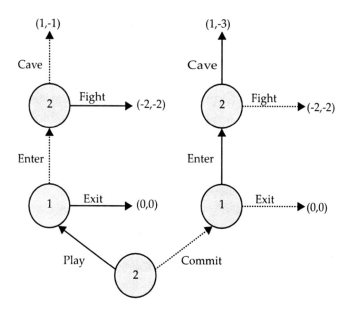

Stackelberg Game Tree

The dashed arrows in the diagram show how to analyze subgame perfection. We start at the end of the game and work backwards towards the beginning. This is called *backward induction, dynamic programming,* or *recursive analysis,* and is a method widely used by economists to analyze complex problems involving the passage of time. We already implicitly used this method when we examined the finitely repeated Prisoner's Dilemma: there we noticed that the final time the game was played it was optimal to *confess.* Here in the *play* subgame if player 2 gets the move, it is best – as shown by the dashed arrow – to *cave.* Working backwards in time knowing player 2 will cave it is best for player 1 to enter. In the *commit* subgame if player 2 gets the move it is best to *fight* since *caving* is now expensive. That means that in the *commit* subgame player 1 should *exit.* Should player 2 commit? If he chooses to *play* we see that player 1 will enter, he will cave and get ⬜1. If he chooses to *commit* player 1 will exit and he will get 0. Consequently it is better to *commit.*

The Stackelberg Game illustrates the two essential components of effective commitment. First, it must be credible. There is no point in my threatening to blow up a hand grenade because I don't like the service at a restaurant – nobody will believe me. In the Stackelberg Game the commitment is credible because it changes the payoff to *caving* from ⬜1 to ⬜3. This could be because of simple pride – having said I am committed to *fighting* I may feel humiliated by *caving.* Or it could be due to a real physical commitment.

A good example of commitment is in the wonderful game-theoretic movie *Dr. Strangelove.* Here it is the Soviet Union attempting to make a commitment to keep the United States from attacking. To make *fight* credible they build a doomsday device. This is an automated collection of gigantic atomic bombs buried underground in the Soviet Union and protected against tampering. If their computers detect an attack on the Soviet Union the doomsday device will automatically detonate and destroy the world. Because the device is proof against tampering the threat is credible: if the United States attacks, nobody, American or Soviet, can prevent the doomsday device from detonating. Devices like this were seriously discussed during the Cold War – and similar devices known as deadman switches have been used in practical wartime circumstances. A deadman switch is a switch that goes off if you die – for example, you remove the pin from a hand grenade, but keep your finger on a spring-loaded trigger. If your enemy kills you, your hand releases the trigger and blows you both to kingdom come. The advantage of such a device is that your enemy is not so tempted to kill you.

One essential element of commitment is that it must be credible. The other is that your opponent must know you are committed. A deadman switch is useless if your enemy doesn't know you have one. A secret doomsday device is equally useless – and that is the heart of the movie *Dr. Strangelove.* The Soviets – apparently not being very bright – activate their doomsday device on Friday with the intention of revealing it to the world on Monday. Unfortunately a mad U.S. general decides to attack the Soviet Union over the weekend... go watch the movie – Peter Sellers plays half a dozen characters and is great as all of them.

And as long as I am on the subject of Peter Sellers, let me mention another fine example of commitment – this from his excellent Pink Panther movies in which Sellers plays the bumbling Inspector Clouseau. Clouseau has an assistant named Kato who is even more bungling than Clouseau himself. In order to provide himself incentive to stay alert against attackers, Clouseau instructs Kato to attack him without warning whenever he is not expecting it. Kato does so – always at especially inopportune moments such as the middle of a phone call or during a particularly elegant dinner date. Naturally – as with all good commitment – after the fact Clouseau has no interest in fighting with

Kato and invariably instructs Kato to go away. Kato, obedient servant that he is, stops fighting – at which point Clouseau sneakily restarts the fight and gives Kato a long lecture about remaining alert. That game-theoretic point is that with a commitment there is always a tension since there is always a temptation not to carry out the threat.

In the end it doesn't matter whether commitments are completely credible – with a truly awful threat just a small chance it will be carried out is enough to serve as an effective deterrent. Thankfully we will never know if the threat of nuclear holocaust which prevented the Cold War from becoming hot was credible.

## Best-Shot

In 1989 Glenn Harrison and Jack Hirshleifer examined subgame perfection in a public goods contribution game called *Best Shot*. There are two players – player 1 moves first and chooses how much to contribute to the common good. After seeing player 1's contribution player 2 decides also how much to contribute. The public benefit is determined by the largest contribution between the two players – that greatest contribution brings a benefit to both players as shown in the table below:

| Contribution | Public Benefit |
|:---:|:---:|
| *$0.00* | $0.00 |
| *$1.64* | $1.95 |
| *$3.28* | $3.70 |
| *$4.10* | $4.50 |
| *$6.50* | $6.60 |

Best Shot Public Benefit

We can analyze this using the tool of best response. If your opponent contributes nothing then selfish you get the difference between your benefit and your contribution as shown below – the best amount to contribute is $3.28 giving you a net private benefit of $0.42.

| Contribution | Net Private Benefit |
|:---:|:---:|
| $0.00 | $0.00 |
| $1.64 | $0.31 |
| $3.28 | $0.42 |
| $4.10 | $0.40 |
| $6.50 | $0.10 |

Best Shot Private Benefit

On the other hand, if your opponent contributes something, your contribution only matters if you contribute more than her, and it is easy to check that it is never worth contributing anything. For example, if your opponent contributes $1.64 you get $1.95; if you contribute $1.64 you still get $1.95; if you contribute more than that your additional benefit is given by:

| Contribution | Additional Benefit |
|:---:|:---:|
| $3.28 | $1.75 |
| $4.10 | $2.55 |
| $6.50 | $4.65 |

Additional Benefit when Opponent Contributes $1.64

so that the additional benefit of contribution is always less than the amount you have to put in.

What does subgame perfection say about this game? If I contribute nothing, then it is best for my opponent to put in $3.28 giving me $3.70. If I contribute anything it is best for my opponent to put in nothing, so I should put in $3.28 giving me a net of $0.42. So it is in fact best for me as the first mover not to contribute and force my opponent to make the contribution. Moreover, when Harrison and Hirshleifer carried out this experiment in the laboratory this is more or less what they found.

In 1992 Prasnikar and Roth carried out a variation on the Harrison and Hirshleifer experiment. They noticed that while Harrison and Hirshleifer had not told participants what the payoffs of their opponent were, they allowed them to alternate between being moving first and second, so implicitly allowed them to realize that their opponent had the same payoffs that they did. To understand more clearly what was going on Prasnikar and Roth forced players to remain in one player role for the entire ten times they got to play the game – that is they either moved first in all matches, or they moved second in all matches. They carried out the experiment under two different information conditions. In the full information condition players were informed of their own payoffs and that their opponent faced the same payoffs. In the partial information condition players were informed only of their own payoffs and were not told that their opponent faced the same payoffs.

In the full information treatment in the final eight rounds as the theory predicts the first mover never made a contribution. In the partial information treatment the bulk of matches also resulted in one player contributing $3.28 and the other $0.00 – but in over half of those matches the player who contributed the $3.28 was the first player rather than – as predicted by subgame perfection – the second player.

On the one hand this is a rather dramatic failure of the notion of subgame perfection. On the other hand – if players don't know the payoffs of their opponent, they can hardly reason what their opponent will do in a subgame, so subgame perfection does not seem terribly relevant to a situation like this. Nor can we expect players necessarily to learn their way to equilibrium – if I move first and kick in $3.28 my opponent will contribute nothing – and I will never learn that had I not bothered to contribute my opponent would have put the $3.28 in for me. We will return to these learning theoretic considerations later.

If we view subgame perfection as a theory of what happens when players are fully informed of the structure of the game we should not expect the predictions to hold up when they are only half informed.

## Information and Subgame Perfection

It is silly to expect subgame perfection when players have no idea what the motivations of their opponents might be. We might, however, hope that the predictions hold up when there is only a small departure from the assumption of perfect information about the game. Unfortunately the theory itself tells us that this is not the case.

In 1988 – before the Harrison and Hirshleifer paper was

published – Drew Fudenberg, David Kreps and I conducted a theoretical study of the robustness of subgame perfect equilibrium to informational conditions. The main point can be illustrated in a simple variation of the Selten Game, the *Elaborated Selten Game* shown below.

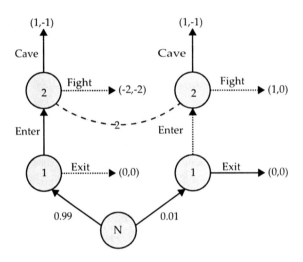

Elaborated Selten Game Tree

This diagram augments the earlier portraits of an *extensive form game* – that is, a game played over time – in two ways. First, it introduces an artificial player called *Nature* labeled N. Nature is not strategic but simply moves randomly. The moves of Nature are labeled with probabilities: in this game with probability 0.99 Nature chooses the Selten game. With probability 0.01 Nature chooses an alternative game. Player 1, who moves first, learns which game is being played. Player 2 who moves second does not. To represent player 2's ignorance we draw a dashed line – an *information set* – connecting the two different nodes at which he might move. This means that while player 2 knows the probabilities with which Nature chooses the game that is played, he is uncertain about which one is actually being played. Notice how a game theorist approaches the issue of "not knowing what game we are playing" by explicitly introducing the possibility that there might be more than one game that can be played.

In this game particular strategies for the two players are shown by the dotted arrows. If Nature chooses the original game, player 1 *exits* – exactly what subgame perfection convinces us that player 1 should not do. If Nature chooses the alternative game player 1 *enters*. If player 2 gets the move he *fights*. Notice that the information set for player 2 means that player 2 – not knowing which eventuality holds – must *fight* regardless of which game is played.

The alternative game has payoffs similar to the Selten game, except that the payoffs to *fight* have been changed from ( –2, –2) to (1, 0). Moreover, given the strategy of player 1, player 2 expects to play sometimes. What does player 2 think when he gets to play? Knowing player 1's strategy, he knows that he is getting to play because Nature chose the alternative game. Hence he knows that it is better to *fight* than to *cave*. But player 1 in the alternative game understands that if she *enters* player 2 will *fight* – and she will get 1 rather than 0 by *exiting* so *entering* is in fact the right thing for player 1 to do. On the other hand in the original game she also knows if she *enters* player 2 will *fight*, so now *exiting* is the right move.

As it happens this Elaborated Selten Game is not usefully analyzed by subgame perfection – it has no subgames! Game theorists have introduced a variety of methods of bringing subgame perfection like arguments to bear on such games: sequential equilibrium, divine equilibrium, intuitive criterion equilibrium, proper equilibrium and hyperstable equilibrium are among the "refinements" of Nash equilibrium that game theorists have considered. However: the equilibrium we have described has the property that it is a *strict Nash equilibrium* meaning that no player is indifferent between their equilibrium strategy and any alternative. A strict Nash equilibrium is "all of the above:" it is subgame perfect, sequentially rational, divine, proper, hyperstable, and satisfies the intuitive criterion. In this sense the prediction of subgame perfection is not robust to the introduction of a small amount of uncertainty about the game being played: the equilibrium play that fails to be subgame perfect – *exit* by player 1 – appears as part of a strict and therefore robust Nash equilibrium. If players are a little unsure of what game they are playing it is merely glib to rule out this possibility. This major theoretical deficiency of the theory of subgame perfection helps explain why it does not do so well in practice.

## Ultimatum Bargaining

One of the famous "failures" of economic theory is in the ultimatum bargaining game. Here one player proposes the division of an amount of money – often $10, and usually in increments of 5 cents – and the second player may accept, in which case the money is divided as agreed on, or reject, in which case neither player gets anything. If the second player is selfish, he must accept any offer that gives him more than zero. Given this, the first player should ask for – and get – at least $9.95. That is the reasoning of subgame perfect equilibrium. Notice, incidentally, that in this game players are fully informed about each other's payoffs.

Not surprisingly this prediction – that the first player asks for and gets $9.95 – is strongly rejected in the laboratory. The table below shows the experimental results of Roth, Prasnikar, Okuno-Fujiwara and Zamir [1991]. The first column shows how much of the $10 is offered to the second player. (The data is rounded off.) The number of offers of each type is recorded in the second column, and the fraction of second players who reject is in the third column.

| *Amount of Offer* | *Number of Offers* | *Rejection Probability* |
|---|---|---|
| *$3.00 or less* | 3 | 66% |
| *$4.75 to $4.00* | 11 | 27% |
| *$5.00* | 13 | 0% |
| U.S. $10.00 stake games, round 10 | | |

Ultimatum Bargaining Experimental Results

Notice that the results cannot easily be attributed to confusion or inexperience, as players have already engaged in 9 matches with other players. It is far from the case that the first player asks for and gets $9.95. Most ask for and get $5.00, and the few that ask for more than $6.00 are likely to have their offer rejected.

Looking at the data a simple hypothesis presents itself: players are not strategic at all they are "behavioral" and fair-minded and just like to split the $10.00 equally. Aside from the fact that this "theory" ignores slightly more than half the observations in which the two players do not split 50-50, it might be wise to understand whether the "economic theory" of rational strategic play has really failed here – and if so how.

The place to start is by looking at the rejections. Economic theory does not demand that players be selfish, although that may be a convenient approximation in certain circumstances, such as competitive markets. Yet it is clear from the rejections that players are not selfish. A selfish player would never reject a positive offer, yet ungenerous offers are likely to be rejected. Technically this form of social preference is called *spite*: the willingness to accept a loss in order to deprive the opponent of a gain. Once we take account of the spite of the second player, the unwillingness of the first player to make large demands becomes understandable.

There is a failure of the theory here, but it is not the fact that the players moving first demand so little. Indeed, from the perspective of Nash equilibrium rather than subgame perfection, practically anything can be an equilibrium: I might ask for only $4.00 thinking you will reject any less favorable offer – and you not expecting to ever be offered less than $6.00 can "hypothetically" reject all less favorable offers at no cost at all. This highlights a key fact about Nash equilibrium – the main problem with Nash equilibrium isn't that it is so often wrong – it is that many times it has little to say. A theory that says "player 1 could offer $5.00... or $2.00... or $8.00" isn't of that much use. Unfortunately the theory does say that all the player 1's must make exactly the same offer as each other. Clearly that is not the case as about half the players offer $5.00 and about half offer less than that.

Recall our rationale for Nash equilibrium: it was a rationale of players learning how to expect their opponent to play. Here if I continually offer my opponent $5.00 I won't learn that they would have been equally likely to accept an offer of $4.75. From the point of view of learning theory Nash equilibrium is problematic in a setting where not everything about your opponent is revealed after each match. We will return to this issue subsequently when we discuss learning theory.

To sum up, the experimental evidence is dramatic: the "theory" predicts the first mover asks for and gets $9.95 or more, while in the experiment nearly half the first movers ask for only $5.00. Yet on closer examination we see that the failure is not so dramatic. The "theory" in question is that of subgame perfection which we know not to be terribly robust. The assumption of selfishness fails, but that is not part of any theory of "rational" play. There is a failure, but it is a different – and more modest – failure. The robust theory of Nash equilibrium is on the one hand weak and tells us little about what sort of offers should be made. On the other hand it predicts all the first movers should make the same offers, and while 90% of them offer in the narrow range between $5.00 and $4.00, they do not all make the same offer.

# Grab a Dollar

In a sense the strongest test of subgame perfection is in a game lasting many rounds – can players indeed carry out many stages of recursive reasoning from the end of such a game? One such game is called *Grab a Dollar*. In this game there are two players and a dollar on the table between them. They take turns either passing or grabbing. Each time a player passes the money on the table is doubled. If as player grabs, she gets the money and the game ends. After a certain number of rounds specified in advance, there is a final round in which the player whose turn it is to move can either grab the money, or leave double the amount to her opponent.

What does subgame perfection say about such a game? Once again we use backward induction to solve the game. In the final round a selfish player should grab. Knowing your opponent will grab in the final round, the player moving next to last should grab right away, so on and so forth. We conclude that in the subgame perfect equilibrium the first player to moves grabs the dollar immediately. It is a little more difficult to show – but the same is true in Nash equilibrium as well.

In 1992 McKelvey and Palfrey tried a variant of this game in the laboratory. Rather than 100% of the money pile, the player who grabbed got only 80% while the loser got the remaining 20%. They also started with $0.50 rather than a dollar. Nevertheless both the subgame perfect equilibrium and indeed all Nash equilibria have the first player to grabbing the $0.50 right away rather than waiting and getting only $0.20 when her opponent grabs in the second round.

In the experiment there were four rounds: the game tree is illustrated below with the options labeled as G1, P1, G2, P2, G3, P3, G4, P4 for grabbing and passing on moves 1, 2, 3 or 4 respectively. Next to each option is shown the fraction of the players who chose that option in brackets. The failure of subgame perfection – and Nash equilibrium – is as dramatic, or perhaps more so, than in ultimatum bargaining. According the theory 100% of people should choose G1, while in fact only 8% of them do.

As in ultimatum bargaining, the place to begin to understand whether the theory has in fact "failed" – and if so, how – is in the final round. Notice that 18% of the player 2's who make it to the final round choose P4 – that is to pass rather than to grab. There is no strategic issue that they face: the game is over – they must decide whether to take $3.20 leaving $0.80 to player 1, or whether to give up $1.60 in order to increase the payment to player 1 by $5.60. Apparently 18% of player 2's are altruistic enough to choose the latter.

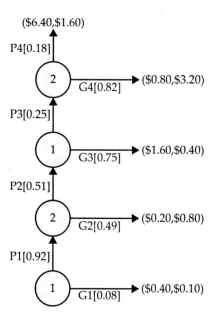

($6.40,$1.60)

P4[0.18]

2 — G4[0.82] → ($0.80,$3.20)

P3[0.25]

1 — G3[0.75] → ($1.60,$0.40)

P2[0.51]

2 — G2[0.49] → ($0.20,$0.80)

P1[0.92]

1 — G1[0.08] → ($0.40,$0.10)

Centipede Game Tree

What may not be so obvious is that 18% of player 2's giving money away at the end of the game changes the strategic nature of play quite a lot. What should a selfish player 1 do on the third move? If he grabs he gets $1.60. If he passes he has an 18% chance of getting $6.40 and an 82% chance of getting $0.80 – that means on average he can expect to earn slightly over $1.80 by passing. In other words – it is better to pass than to grab. The same is true for all the earlier moves – the best thing to do is to stay in as long as you can and hope if you are player 1 you have a kind player 2, and if you are player 2 that you make it to the last round where you can grab.

The puzzle here is not that players are not dropping out fast enough – it is that they are dropping out too soon! Yet perhaps that should not be such a puzzle from the perspective of learning theory: if I am one of the 8% of players who choose to drop out in the first round I will not have the chance to discover that 18% of player 2's are giving money away in the final round.

# 5. You Can Fool Some of the People...

*You may fool all the people some of the time, you can even fool some of the people all of the time, but you cannot fool all of the people all the time.* Abraham Lincoln

What can economic theory reasonably hope to say? Any model is an idealization in which many things that are thought to be relatively unimportant are ignored: decision costs, social preferences, costs of acquiring information, and so forth and so on. Moreover in applied work it is necessary to adopt specific mathematical functions which are at best approximations to an underlying reality. A caricature of *homo economicus* asserts that in the laboratory everyone is selfish and that all the participants understood the instructions. Or more strongly that all students always get all exam questions correct – the falsity of which even academic economists must surely be aware.

Modern economic theory is not such a caricature. As we have seen Nash equilibrium sometimes predicts well – and sometimes does not. Whether a theory that is sometimes right and sometimes wrong is useful depends on whether we can tell in advance when it will be correct. For example, Newtonian mechanics does poorly at speeds close to that of light, but is very useful at lower speeds. It is true that Nash equilibrium is a core concept in modern economic theory. It is, however, the starting point of economic theory, not the ending point – economists have developed a set of tools that enables us to determine when Nash equilibrium is a reasonable approximation and when not.

I have discussed the theory of social preferences and will subsequently discuss learning theory. Besides these specific models, economists have theories that enable us to understand what happens when everyone is a little "irrational" and a few people are very "irrational."

# Approximate Equilibrium

In standard Nash equilibrium it is assumed that every player makes the best choice possible. In 1980 Roy Radner introduced the weaker concept of *approximate Nash equilibrium*: this supposes only that each player makes a relatively good choice. In a correct model for a player to choose her best option given her beliefs is essentially a tautology. Given that models are never correct there is no reason to presume that theoretical players do better than "relatively well."

The idea that players do "well" but not "perfectly" can be found in some of the earliest behavioral criticisms of standard economics. Simon's 1956 notion of *satisficing* behavior – for which he won the Nobel Prize in Economics – supposes that people are satisfied and stop attempting to learn if they achieve a desirable goal that falls short of the very best possible. In Simon's theory this goal is based on historical data about how well the decision-maker has done in the past.

Although it is not widely known modern economics incorporates satisficing concepts in two ways. The first is through the notion of habit formation where preferences change over time as experience is acquired. More on that later. The second is through the notion of approximate optimization.

The idea of approximate optimization is hardly new and scarcely originates either with Simon or Radner. The traditional theory of competitive behavior is a model of approximate optimization. That is, in practice and in any economic model, a trader always has a little bit of market power – even the smallest wheat trader can change prices a tiny bit in her favor by withholding some wheat from the market. But in practice nobody is going to take the time and effort to figure out how to manipulate a market in order to garner a few cents. The theory of competitive behavior supposes that traders ignore the possibility of such small gains.

The use of approximate optimization is also widespread in the modern economic theory of learning. To take two examples: in Foster and Young's 2003 paradigm of the hats it is assumed that a player only try new things if there is evidence of a strategy that works at least a bit better than the status quo. In Fudenberg and Levine [1995] players are assumed to randomize between nearly indifferent alternatives even though this results in slightly less than the optimum payoff. This randomization provides strong protection against an opponent who is cleverer than you are.

The notion of approximate equilibrium is also important for measurement. Given the objective play of other players, and what a player actually did, we can ask "how much more money could that player have earned?" In Nash equilibrium the answer is zero – it is not possible to do better. In approximate Nash equilibrium the answer may be positive – and is often referred to by the Greek letter $\varepsilon$ (pronounced epsilon), which in mathematics is traditionally used to refer to a small number. Notice that modifying Nash equilibrium to allow an $\varepsilon$ loss contains two possibilities. One may be that a player consistently earns a bit less than she might. The other is that she occasionally earns a lot less than she might. That is "all of the people some of the time" and "some of the people all of the time." The former possibility – people occasionally earning a lot less than they might is of particular importance when the population is large, since it implies that a small fraction of the population will be "misbehaving" quite a lot.

Turning back to measurement, $\varepsilon$ is our measure of how much the "true" preferences of the player differ from the preferences that we have written down. So we allow the possibility that the true "payoff" from a choice might be somewhat different than captured by the model, but by no more than $\varepsilon$. In effect $\varepsilon$ is a measure of the approximation we think we made when we wrote down a formal mathematical model of player play, or of the uncertainty we have about the accuracy of that model. To make the long story short, if I write down a model in which the outcome $x$ gives you a payoff of 10 then I allow that payoff to be 10.001, that is $10 + \varepsilon$, but not more.

The measure of "success" for Nash equilibrium should not be whether play "looks like an equilibrium" but whether $\varepsilon$ is small. Take the case of ultimatum bargaining. Fudenberg and Levine [1997] computed the losses to players playing less than a best-response as averaging $0.99 per player per game out of the $10.00 at stake. What is especially striking is that most of the money is not lost by second players to whom we have falsely imputed selfish preferences, but rather by first movers who incorrectly calculate the chances of having their offers rejected. As we have noted, however, a first player who offers a 50–50 split may not realize that she could ask for and get a little bit more without being rejected, nor if she continues to offer a 50–50 split, will she learn of her mistake.

The message here is not that the theory worked well, but rather that the failure of the theory is much less than a superficial inspection suggests. Simply comparing the prediction of subgame perfection to the data indicates that players offered $5.00 when they should have offered $0.05. Yet a more reasonable measure of the success of the theory is that players lose only $0.99 out of the possible $10.00 that they can earn.

## Equilibrium: The Weak versus the Strong

The problem with approximate (or $\varepsilon$) equilibrium is not that it makes inaccurate predictions, but that it makes too many predictions. The ultimatum bargaining game is a perfect example: with $\varepsilon$ = $0.99 half of the offers at $5.00 is an approximate equilibrium – and so are all the offers at $0.05.

Weak predictions are not a good thing in a theory. Yet a theory that is sometimes weak and sometimes strong can be useful if it lets us know when it is weak and when it is strong. When there is a narrow range of predictions – as in the voting game, or in games such as best shot or competitive bidding – the theory is useful and correct. When there is a broad range of predictions such as in ultimatum bargaining the theory is correct, but not as useful.

The role for behavioral economics – if there is to be one – is not to overturn existing theory, but to strengthen it. The evidence is strong that psychological factors are weak compared to economic factors, but in certain types of games that may make a great deal of difference.

## Voting Redux

To get a sense of the limitations of existing theory, it is useful to take a look under the hood of the voting game described earlier. At the aggregate level the model predicts with a high degree of accuracy. However, as anyone who has ever looked at raw experimental data can verify, individual play is very noisy.

The figure below from Palfrey and Levine [2007] summarizes the play of individuals in the voting experiment. Depending on the probability of being pivotal (deciding the election) and on the cost of participation, we can calculate for each player how costly it is to participate. This is shown on the horizontal axis. If – in a given election – the cost is positive the player should not vote; if it is negative then the player should vote. The vertical axis is the actual frequency with which voters participated. The crosses are the results of individual elections. The squares are averages of the crosses for each level of participation cost, and the smooth curve is a theoretical construct described below.

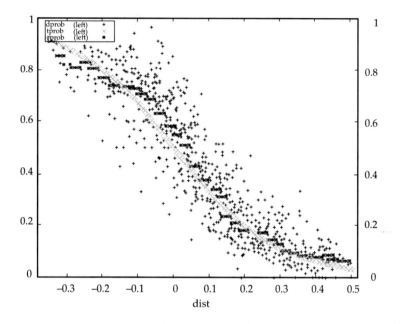

Participation Cost versus Participation Rate

The theory of Nash equilibrium says that we should observe a "best response" function that is flat with the probability of participating equal to one for all negative losses (gains) and flat with a probability of zero for all positive losses. This is far from the case: some players make positive errors, some make negative errors. However in this voting game the errors tend to offset each other. Over voting by one voter causes other voters to want to under vote, so aggregate behavior is not much affected by the fact that individuals are not behaving exactly as the theory predicts. A similar statement can be made about the competitive auction and other games in which equilibrium is strong and robust. By way of contrast in ultimatum bargaining a few players rejecting bad offers changes the incentives of those making offers: they will wish to make lower offers – moving away from the subgame perfect equilibrium, not towards it.

A key feature of the individual level data in the voting game is that behavior is sensitive to the cost of "mistakes." That is, voters are more likely to play "sub-optimally" if the cost of doing so is low. The same is true in ultimatum bargaining: bad offers are less costly to reject than good ones, and are of course rejected more frequently.

# Quantal Response Equilibrium

One response to the fact that in some games such as ultimatum bargaining equilibrium theory makes weak predictions is to try to explicitly model psychological forces to get a more accurate model that can make more exact predictions. A more naïve approach is to ignore psychological forces entirely and just assume that costly deviations from equilibrium are less likely than inexpensive ones. This captures the important fact that when incentives are weak play is less predictable. It leads to a theory known as *quantal response equilibrium* (or QRE) introduced by McKelvey and Palfrey in 1995. It is built on the standard logistic choice model introduced to economics by McFadden in 1980.

QRE supposes that play is somewhat random. It assumes a non-negative numerical parameter usually represented by the Greek letter $\lambda$ (pronounced lambda). This parameter describes how noisy choices are. At one extreme, if $\lambda = 0$ the player simply chooses a strategy at random – there is no strategic behavior. As the parameter $\lambda$ grows large her play approaches the best response of Nash equilibrium. For intermediate values of $\lambda$ strategies with higher payoffs are more likely to be used than those with lower payoffs, but there is still a chance that lower valued alternatives will be chosen.

In a Nash equilibrium players must play optimally given their beliefs and their beliefs must be correct. Similarly, in a QRE players must employ probabilities consistent with $\lambda$ given their beliefs and their beliefs must be correct. Rather than a best response they play a "quantal response."

To give an idea how this theory works in the voting experiment we can estimate a common value of $\lambda$ for all players. The corresponding equilibrium probabilities of play are given by the smooth curve in the figure above. This does an excellent job of describing individual play – although it makes roughly the same predictions for aggregate play as Nash equilibrium.

While QRE is useful in explaining a many experimental deviations from Nash equilibrium in games where Nash equilibrium is weak, it captures only the cost side of preferences. That is, it recognizes – correctly – that departures from standard "fully rational" selfish play are more likely if they are less costly in objective terms, but it does not attempt to capture the benefits of playing non-selfishly. It does not well capture, for example, the fact that under some circumstances players are altruistic, and in others spiteful.

## Selling a Jar of Pennies

Enough theory – would you like to make some money? Here is a surefire way to do it. Put a bunch of pennies in a jar, and get together a group of friends. Then auction off the jar of pennies. You will find if you have about thirty friends that you can sell a $3.00 jar of pennies for about $10.00.

Jar of Pennies

This illustrates an important phenomenon known as the *winner's curse*. Your friends all stare at the jar and try to guess how many pennies there are. Some under guess – they may guess that there are only 100 or 200 pennies. They bid low. Others over guess – they may guess that there are 1,000 pennies or more. They bid high. Of course those who overestimate the number of pennies by the most bid the highest – so you make out like a bandit.

According to Nash equilibrium this shouldn't happen. Everyone should rationally realize that they will only win if they guess high, so they should bid less than their estimate of how many pennies there are in the jar. They should bid a lot less – every player can guarantee they lose nothing by bidding nothing. So in equilibrium, they can't on average lose anything, let alone $7.00.

QRE – by recognizing that there is a small probability that people aren't so rational – makes quite a different prediction. People no doubt perceive that there is some most possible profit they could make by getting the most number of pennies at zero cost. Let's call this amount of utility $\lambda$.

They also perceive that there is some least possible profit by getting a jar with no pennies at the highest possible bid. Let's call that utility $u$. As a formal mathematical theory, QRE says that the ratio of probabilities between two different strategies is a function of $\lambda$ times the difference in utilities – specifically that the ratio of the probability between two bids that give utility $U$, $u$ is $\exp[\lambda (U - u)]$ where exp stands for the exponential function of mathematics. Now whatever is the difference in utility between two strategies it cannot be greater than that between $U$ and $u$. What this means is that the probability of the highest possible bid is always at least some number $\rho > 0$ that may depend on how many bids are possible, but not on how many bidders there are or what strategies they employ.

What happens as the number of bidders grows? Each bidder according to QRE has at least a $\rho$ probability of making the highest possible bid. With many bidders it becomes a virtual certainty that one of the bidders will (unluckily for them) make this high bid, so with enough bidders, QRE assures the seller a nice profit.

## Break Left? Or Right?

The role of approximate equilibrium, of QRE, and of altruism can be seen in analyzing the game of *Matching Pennies*. Each player has a penny, and secretly places it heads up or heads down. If the two pennies match – either both heads or both tails – one player, the matching player, wins both pennies; if the two pennies do not match her opponent wins both pennies.

Matching Pennies is an example of a *zero sum game*: one player's gain is the other's loss. It is not a new game – it is described in Conan Doyle's "The Final Problem" written in 1893. In that story Sherlock Holmes is being pursued by his arch-enemy the brilliant but evil Professor Moriarty. If Holmes can escape to France he wins; if Moriarty can catch Holmes first Moriarty wins. The climactic conclusion of the story finds Holmes on a train bound for Dover and Moriarty pursuing Holmes on another train. The only stop is at Canterbury. If both get off at the same stop Moriarty catches Holmes (the "pennies" match) and Moriarty wins. If they get off at different stops Holmes wins. Despite the supposed brilliance of Holmes and Moriarty, their creator Conan Doyle was not a terribly good game theorist – in the story Holmes reasons that Moriarty thinks he is going to Dover, so he gets off at Canterbury while Moriarty continues to Dover and loses the game. But why does not the supposedly brilliant mathematician

Moriarty understand Holmes reasoning so get off at Canterbury himself? And why does not Holmes anticipating this get off at Dover? Despite the fact that we can repeat this logic endlessly there is a Nash equilibrium – it necessarily requires that players choose randomly. If each has a 50% chance of getting off at Canterbury or Dover, then each has a 50% chance of winning the game no matter what the other player does.

Does that sound realistic? Choosing randomly? The problem of evading capture does not occur only in novels. The best selling book ever released by the RAND Corporation is their 1955 table of random numbers. Folklore has it that at least one captain of a nuclear submarine kept it by his bedside to use in plotting evasive maneuvers. More familiar are sporting events. The soccer player kicking a penalty goal must keep the goal keeper in the dark about whether he will kick to the right, to the left or to the center of the goal; the tennis player must be unpredictable as to which side of the court she will serve to, the football quarterback must not allow the defense to anticipate run or pass, or whether the play will move to the right or the left, and the baseball catcher must keep the batter uncertain as to how his pitcher will deliver the ball. Indeed, at one time in Japan catchers were equipped with small mechanical randomization devices with which to call the pitch – this was later ruled unsporting and banned from play.

In 2001 – in a paper published in what is often viewed as the leading journal in economics – Holt and Goeree studied several variations of Matching Pennies in the laboratory. In the first variation the payoffs were 80 for the winner and 40 for the loser. As in other versions of matching pennies the only Nash equilibrium is for players to randomize 50–50 – and indeed, unlike Holmes and Moriarty – they did just that. The table below shows the theoretical Nash equilibrium of 50% and in parentheses the actual fraction of subjects that chose the corresponding row and column. As you can see it is quite close to 50%.

|  | 50% (48%) | 50% (52%) |
|---|---|---|
| 50% (48%) | 80,40 | 40,80 |
| 50% (52%) | 40,80 | 80,40 |

Matching Pennies: Payoffs and Results

This type of randomization is called a *mixed strategy* Nash equilibrium. Fifty-fifty is a particularly easy strategy to implement, and even though

Conan Doyle couldn't figure it out the experimental participants did. However, the theory of mixed strategy equilibrium is peculiar in that it predicts that each player must randomize so as to make his opponent indifferent. This implies that in a mixed strategy Nash equilibrium each player's play depends only on his opponents' payoffs and not on his own. This can be counterintuitive.

To study randomization Holt and Goeree changed the payoffs by increasing (from 80 to 320) or decreasing (from 80 to 44) the payoff to Player 1 in the upper left corner. In theory this should change Player 2's equilibrium play, but Player 1 should continue to randomize 50-50. The two tables below show the theoretical predictions of Nash equilibrium and in parentheses what actually happened: far from continuing to randomize 50-50 Player 1 played the row containing the highest payoff at least 92% of the time.

|            | 12.5% (16%) | 87.5% (84%) |
|------------|-------------|-------------|
| 50% (96%)  | 320,40      | 40,80       |
| 50% (4%)   | 40,80       | 80,40       |

|            | 87.5% (80%) | 12.5% (20%) |
|------------|-------------|-------------|
| 50% (8%)   | 44,40       | 40,80       |
| 50% (92%)  | 40,80       | 80,40       |

Asymmetric Matching Pennies: Payoffs and Results

As is the case with some of the earlier experiments, the theory here does about as badly as it can: the theory predicts equal probability between the two rows, but the actuality is that one row is played pretty much all the time. However: unlike the other experiments this one involves players who are inexperienced in the sense that they only got to play the game once. From the perspective of learning theory there is no reason we should expect to see a Nash equilibrium. Nevertheless it is interesting to see how well our theoretical tools work in understanding what happened.

The figure below is taken from Levine and Zheng [2010] and illustrates our main concepts. The horizontal axis is the frequency with which Player 1 chooses the *Top* row; the verticle axis the frequency with which Player 2 chooses the *Left* column. The laboratory results are shown by the black dots labeled *Lab Result* with the upper left dot corresponding to the second matrix – the 44 game, and the lower right dot corresponding to the first matrix – the 320 game. The theoretical prediction of Nash equilibrium – that Player 1 (and only Player 1) randomizes 50–50 – are labeled as *Original Nash Equilibrium*.

We consider several different ways of weakening the theory of selfish Nash equilibrium. The first is by computing all the approximate equilibrium in which the losses are no greater than those actually suffered by the participants. This is the light gray shaded region. The second is by computing the QRE corresponding to different levels of noisy decision making. These are the inner curves that begin at the respective Nash equilibria and – as decision making becomes more noisy – move eventually towards the completely random outcome where both players simply make each choice with equal 50% probability. The dark gray region and the outer curves also examine approximate and QRE – but do so under the hypothesis that players are altruistic.

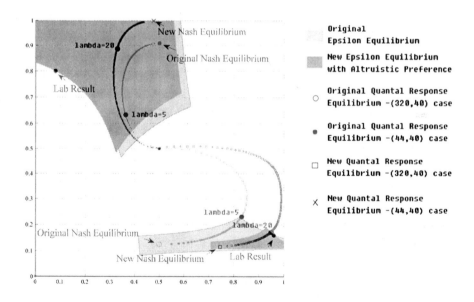

Fraction Playing Left and Top

To understand what this diagram does and does not show, it is useful to start with QRE. One prediction of quantal response is a tendency toward the middle. For example in the 320 game Player 2 plays *Left* in Nash equilibrium 12.5% of the time. Quantal response says that errors in play will push that towards the middle – toward a 50–50 randomization, and indeed we see that in actuality 16% rather than 12.5% of Player 2's play *Left*. This in turn has a substantial impact on the incentives of Player 1: with "too many" player 2's playing *Left*, the best thing for Player 1 to do is to play *Top* and try to get the 320 – and again this is what we see participants do. We see it also in the diagram. As we vary the parameter of noisy choice away from Nash equilibrium and perfect best response we see that QRE play shifts towards to the right – towards the lab result with more Player 1's playing *Top*. Similarly in the 44 game, "too many" player 2's play *Right* – 20% rather than 12.5% – and this tilts the Player 1's towards playing *Down*. Again, the initial effect of increasing the noise parameter is to move the QRE towards the lab result.

Eventually, when the noise becomes too great, QRE approaches a pure 50–50 randomization. What the diagram also shows is that this happens "too soon" in the sense that play in the QRE "starts back" towards 50–50 before it gets to the laboratory result. That effect is much more pronounced in the 44 game than the 320 game.

Next consider altruism. This is potentially important in the 320 game since Player 2 by giving up 40 can increase the payoff of Player 1 by 280 – you don't have to be that generous to take such an opportunity. This also can explain why "too many" Player 2's play *Left*. If we assume a combination of errors due to quantal response and some altruistic players, it turns out we can explain the 320 game quite well, as the curve combining the two effects passes more or less directly through the laboratory result.

In the 44 game the situation is different. Even combining altruistic players with quantal response errors quantitatively we can explain only about half the laboratory result. Here the approximate equilibrium regions can help us understand what is going on. Notice that in the 320 game the approximate equilibrium region while wide is not very tall. While there are many possible strategies by player 1 that are consistent with a relatively small loss, there are very few strategies by player 2: Player 2 must play *Right* with between about 10% and 20% probability. On the other hand, in the 44 game approximate equilibrium indicates we can say little beyond Player 1 should play *Top* more frequently than *Bottom* and Player 2 should play *Right* more frequently than *Left*. The reason for this is not hard to fathom. In the 320 game incentives are relatively strong: by making a wrong choice players can lose between 40 and 280. In the 44 game by making a wrong choices player can lose between 4 and 40. Naturally when incentives are less strong the set of approximate equilibrium is larger and we are less able to make accurate predictions of how players will play.

## Finance Theory and Noise Traders

The notion of approximate equilibrium, especially in the form of QRE, is widely used in experimental economics. But has it taken root in mainstream economics? In the analysis of real economic problems? Like most tools in economics it is applied by economists where it is relevant – where there is empirical and conceptual reason to think that it is important. Nowhere is this more true than in the theory of information in financial markets – and here, in the form of noise traders – it is a key tool of analysis.

Central to any theory of financial markets is the extent to which they are "informationally efficient," meaning how well they incorporate information available to investors about economic circumstances. In a world in which you cannot fool anybody ever the tiniest bit of information would typically be revealed nearly instantaneously – leading to the conundrum that nobody could profit from inside information, and so nobody would bother to acquire any in the first place.

On the other hand – you surely can fool some of the people some of the time – and this idea far from being ignored by economists is the foundation of the modern theory of information in financial markets. It originates in modern form in the dissertation of Anat Admati, published in 1985 in *Econometrica* the leading journal in economic theory. The idea was picked up by Fischer Black. Black's description of noise traders – the small but important irrational component of the market – was published in 1986, and Google assures us there have been some 1328 follow-on papers. Black is hardly an obscure figure: he avoided joining his co-author Myron Scholes on the stand to receive the Nobel Prize in Economics by the time honored tradition of dying too soon. In the event, it would be ridiculous to assert, as many commentators do, that the central finding in modern finance theory is that markets are informationally efficient.

# Conclusion

The chapter started with a quote attributed to Abraham Lincoln: "you cannot fool all of the people all of the time." By way of contrast modern rational expectations theory seems to say "you cannot fool anybody ever." Are economists fools for being slavish disciples of so ridiculous a doctrine? We are not. Modern economic theory is much closer to Abraham Lincoln's point of view than it is to the popular caricature of rational expectations. Approximate equilibrium, quantal response equilibrium and the introduction of noise traders are all widely used methods designed to admit into rational expectations theory the idea that small irrationalities abound. It is fair to say that the basis of modern economics is that most people are rational most of the time. This is far from a slavish devotion to a ridiculous doctrine – it well captures the spirit of Abraham Lincoln.

# 6. Behavioral Theories I: Biases and Irrationality

*It is true that from a behavioral economics perspective we are fallible, easily confused, not that smart, and often irrational. We are more like Homer Simpson than Superman.* Dan Ariely at danariely.com

Economic theory has its weaknesses: the theory of approximate Nash equilibrium may be "correct" but it doesn't always yield strong predictions. Understanding the psychological elements that predominate when economic incentives are weak – understanding the "epsilons" – would be of great value to economics. So you might think that behavioral economics carefully searches through the psychology literature to identify ideas that would help remedy these weaknesses. You would not suppose that behavioral economics was an attempt to remake those areas of economics that are strong and well studied. Nor would you suppose that behavioral economics was an effort to put a mathematical gloss over psychology – perhaps because the salaries for academic economists are much higher than those of psychologists? – in an attempt to develop a theory of what goes inside the mind. That, after all, is a topic of little relevance to economics. And given the propensity of behavioral economists to pick on the most trivial deviations from standard theory, you would imagine that behavioral theories are subject to deep and careful scrutiny by behavioral economists. For the most part you would be wrong.

Behavioral economics is hard to define. Because it is a terribly trendy term some research that antedates the invention of the word and has little to do with psychological theory or data – such as learning theory – is sometimes referred to also as "behavioral." Sometimes it seems as if anything these days besides the purest of rational models sells itself as "behavioral."

To get a handle on what behavioral economics is, let's turn to some self identified behavioral economists. George Akerlof in his 2001 Nobel lecture lists a number of topics he regards as "behavioral": reciprocity, fairness, identity, money illusion, loss aversion, herding, and procrastination. A 2009 article by Stefano DellaVigna – in the very mainstream *Journal of Economic Literature* – provides a nice outline of the issues examined in behavioral economics as well as some of the evidence. DellaVigna lists three main categories of topics as "behavioral": non-standard preferences, incorrect beliefs, and systematic biases in decision making.

DellaVigna lists three types of non-standard preferences: time preferences, risk preferences and social preferences. Akerlof's procrastination along with what is known as *present bias* fall into the category of time preferences. Akerlof's loss aversion, the psychological theory of decision making under uncertainty called *prospect theory* along with what are known as the Allais and Rabin paradoxes fall into the category of risk preferences. Akerlof's reciprocity and fairness are examples of social preferences – it means simply that people care about the fate of other people.

DellaVigna discusses several ways in which people systematically have incorrect beliefs. One is that people are systematically overconfident; that they tend to put too much reliance on small samples, and that they systematically underestimate their ability to adapt to future circumstances. Akerlof's money illusion, presumably, is also an example of incorrect beliefs.

Finally, DellaVigna lists a number of systematic biases in decision making. None will come as a great shock to anyone with a modicum of common sense. *Framing* refers to the fact that the answer often depends on the way a question is framed. What is 2.2 times 75? How about 2 times 75 plus 10%? I find the latter question much easier to answer than the first, although they are in fact the same question. Additional biases DellaVigna discusses are the fact that we have limited attention, that our current emotions have an impact on our decisions and that we respond to social pressure – the identity and herding that Akerlof refers to.

## Some History

The effort to incorporate more "psychological" elements into economic models is not new. The description of this effort as "behavioral economics" seems to have come into use to describe this sub-genre of economics only in the last decade or so.

To reiterate a point made in the introduction Thorstein Veblen was criticizing economics for excessive use of the notion of rationality in 1898. More recently several Nobel Prizes in Economics have been given for what can only be described in modern terms as behavioral economics. One – the aforementioned George Akerlof – wasn't awarded the prize for his behavioral research, but rather his research on models of rational agents in "markets where sellers of products have more information than buyers about product quality." Since "he showed that low-quality products may squeeze out high-quality products in such markets, and that prices of high-quality products may suffer as a result" one might think that he is aware that traditional economic models can result in market outcomes that appear to be "behavioral" in nature.

Several earlier Nobel Prizes in Economics were for work that was explicitly "behavioral": that awarded to Herbert Simon in 1978 as well as that awarded to Daniel Kahneman – a psychologist – in 2002. In both cases, of course, the work for which the prize was awarded took place years before. In Kahneman's case the work was conducted with Amos Tversky who was ineligible for the prize in 2002 on account of his having died in 1996.

I previously discussed the work of Herbert Simon and his invention of the alternative to optimization called *satisficing*. This supposes that, rather than optimizing, people simply try to do "reasonably" well. Although the model has never been widely used in economics, I explained how the basic idea has become part of mainstream economics through the notion of approximate optimization. Likewise Simon's notion of a target that grows and declines based on past experience is also widely used both in learning theory and in preference theory where it reappears in the widely used habit formation model.

Kahneman and Tversky, along with Richard Thaler, pointed out a wide variety of psychological paradoxes with standard decision theory. One of them – the Allais paradox – was first pointed out by Maurice Allais in 1953. They have also pointed out a wide range of other anomalies or supposed anomalies most of which emerge in an experimental setting. This includes framing – people making different choices based on how the problem is presented, as well as systematic biases in decision-making. Kahneman and Tversky are also responsible for a theoretical effort to remedy some of these problems – a decision-making theory called prospect theory. This differs from the standard economic theory of expected utility in two ways. First, it supposes *loss aversion* – that people care about gains and losses relative to some (unspecified) starting point. Second, it supposes that people systematically overestimate low probabilities and underestimate high probabilities. This theory has had no impact on economics whatsoever but has become the gold-standard for psychologists.

More recently Matt Rabin, an economist and winner of the highest award given by the American Economic Association – the John Bates Clarke medal – has explored the fact that people are not always selfish, but often altruistic or spiteful, and in many instances care about fairness. He also pointed out a considerably bigger problem with expected utility theory than the Allais paradox, a problem now called the Rabin paradox.

Notice that there is a sense in which behavioral economics *is* mainstream: many of the critics of existing theory and practice have had their work recognized by traditional honors such as the Nobel Prize and the John Bates Clarke medal.

## Framing and Anchoring

Are preferences unstable as some behavioral economists such as Dan Ariely would have us believe? One of the key paradoxes that drives behavioral economics is what is called the *framing effect*. DellaVigna, for example, lists this as an important systematic bias in decision making. Framing refers to the fact that the answer to a question often depends on the way the question is framed. As I pointed out above 2.2 times 75 is a more difficult question than what is 2 times 75 plus 10% although they are in fact the same question. By the same token, if I ask you whether you would prefer to vote for the candidate who dropped out of Harvard or the one who founded Microsoft, you will probably choose the latter, even though both are Bill Gates. Put this way, framing is hardly controversial. As always the devil is in the details.

Closely connected to the framing effect is the idea in prospect theory of loss aversion – that losses relative to the status quo are what matters. One variation on this theme is what is called the *endowment effect*. This asserts that the way in which you value an item depends on whether you are buying it or selling it. Precisely, we can try to determine what is called *willingness to pay* for an item, which is just what it sounds like, and *willingness to accept* payment for an item, which is the opposite. For example, if we ask people how much they are willing to pay for a coffee cup they will state a relatively low value; if we give them a coffee cup and ask how much they will sell it for they will state a relatively high value.

On the surface this is not much of a paradox: we all know to buy low and sell high. However: the elicitation of values is done using a method called the Becker-DeGroot-Marschak [1964] elicitation procedure. A willingness to pay or accept payment is stated, and then a random draw is made. If the random draw is lower than the stated value (in the willingness to pay case) then the item is sold at the randomly drawn price. If the draw is higher than the stated value then no transaction takes place.

Is it obvious to you that when this procedure is used that the unambiguously best course of action is to bid your true value and not buy low and sell high? It is true, and subjects are often informed of this fact. So: is there a paradox here, as some behavioral economists and psychologists would argue, or, returning to the theme of which kinds of mistakes are most likely, is it simply the case that people have trouble understanding a complex and unfamiliar procedure?

The answer is that people don't understand the procedure: Plott and Zeiler [2004] show that if subjects are well trained in understanding the elicitation procedure – that is, they clearly understand that the best thing to do is to state their true value – then there is no difference between willingness to pay and willingness to accept payment.[1] If the observation that people have trouble understanding complex decisions and sometimes make mistakes is "behavioral" then we scarcely need experimental evidence to prove the point – the fact that students get exam questions wrong should be proof enough that people fall short of complete and total rationality.

Another case in point is the *anchoring effect*. This says that we can get people to bid pretty much anything by telling them an irrelevant number before they submit their bid. This was documented in an experiment of Ariely, Loewenstein and Prelec [2003]. They first asked people to record the final digits of their social security number, then solicited their willingness-to-pay for various items. They discovered that people who recorded high numbers bid high, and vice versa. The only problem with this experiment appears to be an artifact that can't be replicated. Fudenberg, Levine and Maniadis [2011] carried out a similar experiment

---

1    At least for objects such as coffee cups – when the objects are lotteries the situation is less clear.

in which subjects were asked to record random numbers then solicited their willingness to accept. The table below reports their findings, in particular, the median willingness to accept for those who recorded the lowest and highest random numbers.

| | Academic Planner | Cordless Keyboard | Financial Calculator | Designer Book | Milk Chocolates | Cordless Mouse |
|---|---|---|---|---|---|---|
| Lowest 20% of random numbers | 5 | 35 | 10 | 10 | 4 | 25 |
| Highest 20% of random numbers | 7.5 | 30 | 24 | 15 | 6.5 | 20 |

Median Willingness to Accept: Size of Payment

The magnitudes are far less than found in Ariely, Loewenstein and Prelec [2003]; the cordless keyboard and cordless mouse go in the wrong direction. They are also quite robust, for example, if willingness-to-pay is elicited, rather than willingness to accept the results are quite similar.

# A Short History of Social Preferences in Economics

I'm not going to talk extensively about social preferences – I've talked about it already and there isn't anything particularly "non-standard" about it. "Externalities" in preferences, meaning that people care about other people's consumption is hardly new in economics, nor is the assumption that people are selfish a core precept of modern economic theory.

So let me instead give an extremely brief history of social preferences in economic thought. We can start with Edgeworth's theory of competitive equilibrium in 1881. He explicitly allowed for the possibility that consumers might have preferences over each other's consumption. Moving ahead to 1978, Goldman wrote about gift giving equilibria and economic efficiency: this was published in the mainstream *Journal of Economic Theory*. Trout Rader's 1980 paper "The Second Theorem of Welfare economics when Utilities are Interdependent" was also published in that journal, and made his reputation as an outstanding economist. In more recent years we have contributions such as Kranich's 1988 work in the *Journal of Public Economics*. Or even more recently in 2011 there is the work of Dufwenberg et al. from which I stole this history.

While social preferences are interesting for a variety of reasons, few have suggested that they are terribly important to the things that concern economists: economic crises, for example. The exception is George Akerlof who in his Nobel lecture talks about a theory called *efficiency wages* as a source of economic fluctuations. Efficiency wages says that employers pay workers more than their "market wage" so that they will fear being fired. To make this work employers have to ration jobs – they must turn away some people who would work at this supra-market wage. These people are described as *involuntarily unemployed* – meaning they are willing and able to work at the prevailing wage. There are two explanations of why employers might do this. One, discussed by Shapiro and Stiglitz in 1984, is a perfectly standard economic explanation. Workers effort is unobserved, so to get them to work hard they have to be punished – that is fired – if they are caught shirking. But if workers are paid sufficiently little they won't care if they are fired, so they must be paid a premium for the threat to be effective. The other explanation is "behavioral." Workers will have good feelings (social preferences) towards their employer if they are paid a bonus over the market and bad feelings if they are not.

I don't really want to get into a debate about this: no doubt both things are true – and likely not very quantitatively significant. But the key thing is: as far as economic research has been able to tell – with many efforts and noble failures – unemployment is a symptom rather than a cause of business cycles. As best we can tell – and that is pretty well – it is fluctuations in productivity, in asset prices and in investment that drives the business cycle, not changes in the labor market.

## Incorrect Beliefs and Systematic Biases

In his survey DellaVigna lists several ways in which people systematically have incorrect beliefs. One is that people are systematically overconfident, that they tend to put too much reliance on small samples, and that they systematically underestimate their ability to adapt to future circumstances. To this we may add Akerlof's money illusion.

Money illusion basically means that if your salary goes up by 10% and prices go up by 10% you feel richer – despite the fact that you can't afford any more than you could originally. Of course we may be more aware of changes in our salaries than changes in other prices. Regardless, the main implication that Akerlof and others point to is what is called *price stickiness*: when demand falls there is a tendency not to lower prices. The evidence as to whether this is true is mixed, to say the least. But true or false, it can scarcely be said that economists have ignored the possibility – price stickiness is the foundation of what is called the *New Keynesian* macroeconomics. The idea is that prices are listed on menus and there is a (likely quite small) cost of printing a new menu. We find, for example, that Mankiw's 1985 paper on menu costs is cited by around 900 follow-on papers. It was published in the very mainstream *Quarterly Journal of Economics*, and Mankiw himself was the Chairman of the Council of Economic Advisors – under President George W. Bush, no less!

Turning from money illusion to systematic overconfidence it is not that easy to tell if people are genuinely overconfident or if they merely want the world to believe they are confident. After all, there are many advantages in other people believing you are capable – and if you do not act confident, other people will lack confidence in you. Everybody knows that the captain of the sinking ship must act as if everything is under control. Moreover – we are all familiar with Lake Wobegon where all the children are above average – and we laugh because we understand that everyone cannot be above average. Except – they can be. Sobel and Santos-Pinto pointed this out in an article in the *American Economic Review* in 2005.

How can everyone be above average? Ability and capability are measured on many dimensions. Take driving for example – how fast can you drive? How well do you avoid accidents? How well can you park? Can you corner? And so forth and so on. So any question about "how good a driver do you think you are" implies a value judgement about the relative important of all these different dimensions of driving. Naturally I tend to excel at those elements of driving I think are important – I drive fast and corner well, but have a lot of accidents and I'm a lousy parker. Therefore according to what I think is important I am above average driver. Of course you probably think that avoiding accidents and parking well are important, so naturally you are good at that. Of course according to your values you are also an above average driver. The point is undoubtedly we can be – and are – all above average.

Another systematic bias is that we do not understand properly the laws of probability applied to small numbers. That is, many people if a coin is flipped several times and comes up heads each time will say that the coin is now "due" to come up tails – although this is not true.

A less clear-cut bias is that people appear not to use prior information effectively. For example, if we describe Steve as "shy and withdrawn, invariably helpful, but with little interest in people or the world of reality..." and so forth then ask people whether he is more likely to be a librarian than a salesman, many people will say librarian. Given the fact that there are vastly many more salesmen than librarians this is not in fact terribly likely. However, this finding is controversial, because in settings involving real decisions people seem to account for prior information more appropriately. For example, police investigating the homicide of a woman rarely dismiss the husband as a suspect merely because he is meek in manner.

DellaVigna argues that we systematically underestimate our ability to adapt. For example, academics who do not get tenure find that it makes them much less unhappy than anticipated. This may well be true. If so it would mean, among other things, that people may over-react to economic crises that force them to change their way of life. What exactly we can do about this is unclear. Trumpeting from the rooftops "life isn't so bad – look for another line of work" probably isn't going to win many political campaigns.

DellaVigna also points out that we have limited attention. We are surrounded by facts and can scarcely incorporate them all into our beliefs in some magical and efficient way. For the most part this is innocuous – but work especially by Chris Sims on "rational inattention" indicates that the impact of economic shocks may be muffled by our inability to immediately recognize what is happening.

Finally, DellaVigna mentions that decisions depend on emotions. We are far more likely to buy that expensive car relaxing in a comfortable chair sipping coffee than if we are standing in the freezing rain – a fact that every car dealer knows. However, besides car dealers and other sales people – how this observation might enable us to build better economic institutions is uncertain.

# Identity

In his survey, DellaVigna suggests that the fact that we respond to social pressure is a systematic bias. Basically, we are more likely to give the answer we think everyone else is likely to give. This is not so clearly behavioral – preferences for conformity have been part and parcel of economics at least since Duesenberry's work on consumption in 1949. I suppose calling this "behavioral economics" gives a modern sheen to an oft-investigated topic. Certainly it forms the center-piece of Akerlof's Nobel lecture discussion of the role of identity in reinforcing poverty.

> ...behavioral economics also offers insight on the most enduring macroeconomic problem facing the United States: the disparity in income and social condition between the majority white population and the African American minority... The black poverty rate of 23.6% in 2000 was roughly triple the white rate of 7.7... the problems of the poorest African-Americans go beyond mere poverty. They include extraordinarily high rates of crime, drug and alcohol addiction, out-of-wedlock births, female-headed households and welfare dependency...
>
> Because standard economic theory, in our view, is incapable of explaining such self-destructive behavior, Rachel Kranton and I have developed models, based upon sociological and psychological observations to understand the persistence of African-American disadvantage. Our theory stresses the role of identity and the decisions that individual make about who they want to be. In our theory... dispossessed races... face a Hobbesian choice. One possibility is to choose an identity that adapts dominant culture. But such an identity is adopted with the knowledge that full acceptance by members of the dominant culture is unlikely. Such a choice is also likely to be psychologically costly to oneself since it involves being someone "different"; family and friends, who are also outside the dominant culture are likely also to have negative attitudes towards a maverick...

Let us start by acknowledging that no social problem of this magnitude has an easy solution. Low education and ambition are undoubtedly passed from parent to child. While some succeed in overcoming this handicap of early childhood, far more do not. I do not imagine that any economist, behavioral or otherwise would be likely to dispute this point.

The story Akerlof tells is a version of what is called the *herding model* – in the simplest version this just says that people follow the crowd. As far as I can tell there is nothing irrational about this. If we care about our social interaction with people – if we want to have friends, and I don't see anything particularly irrational in that – then the game theorist in me feels impelled to point out that we can have coordination equilibria in which everyone conforms, and anyone who does not conform is excluded, including those foolish enough not to exclude non-conformists.

However, before worrying about identity and crowd following, we might also want to start with more basic questions about poverty and rationality. For example: is drug use irrational when you are poor? If the alternatives are to live in miserable poverty or escape to drug-induced fantasy – well the fantasy doesn't sound so bad to me. Drug use is hardly particular to poor African Americans. Not surprisingly poor whites who live in rural areas of the southern United States are the center of the modern methamphetamine epidemic.

Is criminal activity irrational? From an economic point of view it is – criminals don't do that well financially. But when we factor in the excitement of being a criminal the choice is less obvious. Certainly if I grew up in a poor neighborhood, being part of a criminal gang would have a lot of appeal. With respect to out-of-wedlock births, female-headed households and welfare dependency: it would be useful to keep in mind that the government will give you money if you are poor and have dependent children – unless of course you are married.

Lack of education is certainly an important source of poverty. This in turn depends on the effort put into education. Does a student give up social activity to study hard? Does the parent give up luxuries to pay for the child's education? Standard economics suggests that whether this is so depends on incentives. In the case of the African American community, do not forget that until the mid-1960s African Americans were excluded from many educational opportunities by force of law. The story of the great American mathematician – and hero to all economists – David Blackwell is a striking case in point. After finishing his Ph.D., Blackwell was turned down for an assistant professor job at Berkeley (University of California) for one reason and one reason only: he was African American. If I were a young African American I would certainly be inclined to think: if one of the greatest mathematicians of the century with all of his education can't get a job – what hope is there for me?

The negative discrimination of the 1960s eventually turned into positive discrimination called affirmative action. If negative discrimination made it rational for African Americans not to invest in education, why did not reverse discrimination result in a flowering of education? Perhaps as Akerlof suggests the problem lies in some sort of social identity.

I am not unsympathetic to that idea, but I think it is useful to look more closely at the consequences of discrimination. Does reverse discrimination result in the flowering of education? The reputation in educational institutions held by the English upper class and rich Saudis speaks for itself. Does negative discrimination necessarily discourage education? When my father attended Harvard University shortly after World War II, he was quite lucky to do so – he is Jewish, and at that time Harvard had explicit Jewish quotas. The affirmative action in favor of African Americans generally discriminates against other races and social groups – not so much whites as Asians. Yet these other groups who were discriminated against put enormous effort into education.

Let's step back for a moment, and try to view all this through the lens of common sense. First, African Americans were heavily discriminated against and provided low effort in attaining education. Later, they were discriminated in favor of and – like other groups who were discriminated in favor of – they provided low effort. By way of contrast Jews and Asians who were mildly discriminated against provided high effort. Could it be that both heavy discrimination against and favorable discrimination provide incentives for low effort, while middle levels of discrimination against provide incentives for high effort? That would reconcile all these facts without recourse to identity or social pressure, or indeed anything "behavioral."

To show how an economist would approach this, I will build a simple mathematical model of discrimination and effort in education. Suppose a student makes an effort $f$ and draws a test score $s$. If the score exceeds a threshold $t$ the student is admitted to college. A very simple model hypothesizes that the test score is drawn from what is called an exponential distribution with mean equal to the level of effort – so that higher effort results, on average, in higher test scores. Under this assumption we can compute that the probability of admission is $\rho = \exp(-t/f)$.

To model incentives, suppose that 0 is the reward for not being admitted to college, that $w$ is the reward for success and that the cost of providing a unit of effort is 1. Then the objective function or "utility" of a student is given by reward times the probability of reward, minus the expense of effort: $v(f) = w \exp(-t/f) - f$.

I'm afraid the next bit is kind of technical. The bottom line is that if students choose the "optimal" or "rational" level of effort, then the level of effort as a function of the probability of admission is $f = -w\rho \log \rho$, the so-called "entropy" function much beloved of physicists. If that is enough for you, please skip to the next paragraph. Otherwise, observe that the first derivative of the objective function is $v' = \omega \exp(-t/f)(-t/f^2) - 1$. Now I will do a brief study of this function so that you can picture it in your mind. As effort goes to zero (that is, the student procrastinates all the time) $f \to 0$ we can use L'Hospital's rule to show that $v' \to 0$, and that as effort grows (the student spends more and more hours studying) $f \to \infty$ we have $v' \to -1$, that is, this function is bounded. The second derivative is $\omega \exp(-t/f)(-t/f^3)(-t/f - 2)$ which is initially positive for values of effort that satisfy $f < t/2$, then changes sign once and becomes negative. The objective function, in other words, is single-peaked – think of the shape of a volcano or other isolated mountain. What this means is that the optimum is the unique solution of the first order condition $v' = \omega \exp(-t/f)(-t/f^2) - 1 = 0$ which may be rewritten as $f = \omega \exp(-t/f)(t/f)$. Intuitively, there exists only one level of effort that gives the maximum possible level of utility to the student. We can further rewrite the "optimal" level of effort in terms of the probability of admission as $f = -\omega\rho \log \rho$.

What does the entropy function $f = -\omega\rho \log \rho$ look like? It is always non-negative, when $\rho = 0$ it is zero, and when $\rho = 1$ it is also zero, and in between it has a single peak. Intuitively, what this means is that if the probability of admission is either very high or very low, you should provide little effort (heavy discrimination against, or heavy discrimination in favor) and for intermediate chances of admission – you should provide a lot of effort.

We can pit this theory against reality. Prior to 1995 the University of California discriminated in favor of African Americans. In that year it abolished discrimination based on racial considerations. Bearing in mind when you actually apply to college, it is a bit late to change your effort level, we would expect that the immediate effect of ending affirmative action would be to lower acceptance rates for African American students. However, over a longer period of time, we would expect the effort level of younger students to adjust upwards, so that after an initial drop, over time, admissions rates would start go up. A report of the Office of the President of the University of California in 2003 provides the relevant data. And indeed we see that after an initial four-year decline in admission rates, they begin to go back up again.

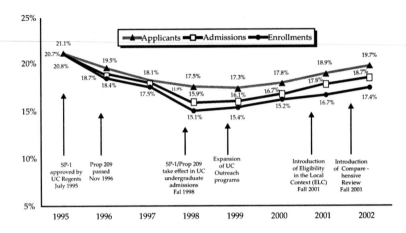

Underrepresented Minority Applicants, Admissions and Freshman Enrollments
Before and After Elimination of Race-Conscious Policies in UC Admissions
UC Systemwide Data, 1995 to 2002

## Summing Up

As the introduction to this section says and the previous chapters
show – economic theory has its weaknesses. Unfortunately, as this chapter
and the next show, behavioral economics is driven by the concerns of
psychologists not economists, so does little to remedy the weaknesses of
economic theory.

It is easy to be dismissive of standard theory on the grounds that
clever theorists can explain anything. It is equally fashionable to complain
that economic theories have too many explanatory variables – which for
behavioral economists is a case of the pot calling the kettle black. These
critiques miss a deeper point: are people functional in the decisions they
make or not? In fact people (and for that matter, as we will see, pigeons)
are quite clever. Seemingly dysfunctional behavior is often quite sensible
when the circumstances and incentives are understood properly – but
circumstances and incentive can be subtle. The evolutionary biology
literature is a case in point – a lot of very strange seeming behavior by
animals – changing sexes over the lifecycle, for example – makes quite a lot
of sense when properly understood.

There is a line between understanding something that is truly
functional and rationalizing everything we see. In the end, though, the
test isn't that hard. A good definition of a *behavioral mistake* is – when

we explain to people why they are doing the problem wrong they agree and change their behavior. If their behavior was functional in the first place they aren't terribly likely to do this. My complaint against a lot of "behavioral economics" is that there is such an obsession with people being dysfunctional that not only are the subtle reasons why behavior may be functional overlooked – but often the extremely obvious reasons are overlooked as well. The example of procrastination in the next chapter is one of many.

Let me conclude with a suggestion for behavioral economists. If there is something glaringly missing from economics it is a theory of imagination. Imagination plays a key role in our preferences: besides the obvious things such as novels and movies, our imagination contributes to our enjoyment of goods and services in many dimensions. At the same time imagination is crucial to innovation – it is the driving force behind our ever increasing production and the material benefits that brings. Yet there is a trade-off in imagining things. Living a life entirely of fantasy – pretending we are Nobel Prize winning scientists and Olympic athletes – is not terribly satisfying. Useful imagination must be grounded in reality. The serious research of understanding the trade-off between fantasy and reality may not be as much fun as fantasizing that people are irrational – but in the long run it provides greater benefits.

# 7. Behavioral Theories II: Time and Uncertainty

The previous chapter discussed various irrationalities and biases alleged by behavioral economists. Much of the work in behavioral economics, however, has focused on the elements of time and uncertainty. Unlike the biases of the previous chapter – which generally attack issues that are not of great interest to economists – time and uncertainty lie at the very heart of modern economics. So let us examine these topics from the behavioral point of view.

## Present Bias

One distinguished critic of "standard economics" is David Laibson of Harvard who had drawn the profession's attention to the phenomenon known as *present bias*. As an example, most people given a choice between $175 today and $192 in four weeks time will take the immediate payoff of $175. On the other hand given a choice of $174 in 26 weeks time and $192 in 30 weeks time (also four weeks later) most people will take the $192. The data from Keren and Roelofsma [1995] below puts specific numbers to this.[1]

---

1   This experimental result is confirmed by Weber and Chapman [2005], and discussed in Halevy [2008], who proposed an objective function that is consistent with these choices. Note that the experiment was in Dutch Florins. I converted from Dutch Florins to U.S. Dollars using an exchange rate typical of the early 1990s of 1.75 Florins per Dollar.

| Scenario | Choices | Fraction Making Choice |
|----------|---------|------------------------|
| 1 | $175 now | 0.82 |
| | $192 in 4 weeks | 0.18 |
| 2 | $175 in 26 weeks | 0.37 |
| | $192 in 30 weeks | 0.63 |

Fraction of People Making Choice[2]

This type of behavior has been long established in psychology, for example, in the 1996 work of Green and Myerson. Notice that the fact that people discount the future is present in virtually all of economic thought. Yet present bias violates the standard economic model in which people discount the future using geometric weights.

The first thing to observe is that this type of present bias is only apparently inconsistent with the standard model of geometric discounting. A number of economists such as Fernandez-Villaverde and Mukherji [2003] have pointed out that in practice we have much more knowledge of our immediate desires than our future desires. That is: some of us could really use some money today rather than in four weeks time and we know it. Still, many fewer of us know that twenty-six weeks from now we will be in desperate need of a cash infusion. In the presence of uncertainty we may well observe what appears to be a "present bias" even with standard *homo economicus*.

Present bias raises yet another issue: if we really feel today that we'd rather have $192 in thirty weeks time than $175 in twenty six weeks time but, given the choice, twenty six weeks from now rather than today would choose the $175 then there is a conflict between our current self and our future self. So given a choice today between $175 in twenty six weeks, $192 in thirty weeks, or being allowed to wait and make the decision twenty six weeks from now – some of us would choose the $192 over the option of waiting. This can't be due to uncertainty about our future desires: in that case the best thing to do is wait and see what they are. A single rational decision maker would always prefer the flexibility of waiting, so *self-commitment* – intentionally limiting our future options – is not consistent with standard economic models.

---

2    The sample consists of 60 individuals.

It is not so hard to think of examples of self-commitment. The Nobel Prize winning game theorist Tom Schelling tells a story of trying to stuff a carton of cigarettes down the garbage disposal in the middle of the night. Given the likely effect on the garbage disposal this cannot have been a good idea – but the reason for it was sound enough; he was afraid of facing the temptation of smoking and wanted to take it off the table. A less obvious example can be found in DellaVigna and Malmendier's 2006 study of health club memberships. People who chose long-term memberships rather than pay per visit paid on average $17 per visit against a $10 per visit fee. Leaving aside the hassle factor of availability of lockers and the need to pay each visit, we can agree that this is some evidence that people are trying to make a commitment to attending the health club.

As we said, in the idealized world usually studied by economists, there is no need for a single decision-maker ever to commit. In reality we often choose to make commitments to avoid future behavior we expect to find tempting but with bad long-term consequences: the drug addict who locks himself in a rehab center would be another obvious example. The long-term membership in a health club has a similar flavor. Skipping a workout can be tempting but has bad long-term consequences for health. Having to pony up $10 makes it easier to find excuses to avoid going.

There is little new under the sun: the economist Richard Strotz was studying problems of self-commitment in the rather mainstream *Review of Economic Studies* back in 1955. However the type of models he proposed were not widely used until the "behavioral economics revolution." Two models that have come into widespread use are called respectively *hyperbolic* and *quasi-hyperbolic* discounting (also known as the beta-delta model) – as opposed to the more ordinary and familiar geometric sort of discounting. David Laibson's [1997] paper examining the consequences of hyperbolic discounting models for consumption behavior – a topic of great interest to economists, although quite possibly nobody else – was published in the also mainstream *Quarterly Journal of Economics* and has been cited some 1543 times, so cannot be said to have been overlooked. The only problem with the model is that it predicts that present bias should not depend on whether or not the reward is uncertain. Unfortunately this is not the case.

| Scenario | Choices | Probability of reward[3] | |
|----------|---------|:---:|:---:|
| Scenario | | **1.0 (60)** | **0.5 (100)** |
| 1 | $175 now | 0.82 | 0.39 |
| 1 | $192 in 4 weeks | 0.18 | 0.61 |
| 2 | $175 in 26 weeks | 0.37 | 0.33 |
| 2 | $192 in 30 weeks | 0.63 | 0.67 |

Fraction Making Choice with Uncertain Reward

Turning back to the data from Keren and Roelofsma [1995] as displayed in the table above – they examined what happened to preference reversals when there was only a 50% chance of getting the money.

A fair summary of the data is that when the chance of reward is only 50% people behave pretty much the same way with respect to both the present and future reward as they do with a certain future reward. If a non-standard model of discounting is needed to understand the first column, the standard model is needed to understand the second. This makes it hard to argue that the "behavioral" model is better than the standard one.

While it isn't at all obvious that present bias has much to say about why we have economic crises or some countries are so poor, the topic has still gained the interest of economists, even economists such as the Princetonian pair Faruk Gul and Wolfgang Pesendorfer who are strongly declared opponents of any notion of behavioral. In 2001 the two wrote a paper proposing that people have preferences over menus – lists of which options will be available – that exhibit a preference for commitment. Dekel, Lipman and Rustichini proposed a similar model at about the same time. Variants of these models including models of internal conflict called self-control models are a major topic of ongoing research. For example, the enormously distinguished and mainstream economists Drew Fudenberg and David Levine wrote about self-control models in the *American Economic Review* in 2006 and again in *Econometrica* in 2012.

---

3    Sample sizes are in parentheses.

Models of *self-control* may reasonably be described as behavioral: they postulate that rather than a single decision maker each of us has several conflicting selves and that the resolution of internal conflict leads to our final decisions. These models were pioneered by behaviorists: Shefrin and Thaler in 1981 and Ainslie in 2001. They have an obvious role in explaining things such as impulsive behavior and drug addiction. On the other hand, while I personally think that these types of models have a great deal to say about behavior – there is still a need for caution in interpreting what people do.

The fact is that a lot of behavior that is commonly thought to be impulsive – spur of the moment, giving in to temptation and taking immediate gratification at the expense of the future – is nothing of the sort. Gambling and sexual behavior are common examples of supposedly impulsive behavior. Nevertheless this so called "impulsive" behavior – giving in to temptation – is often anything but. Take Eliot Spitzer who lost his job as governor of New York because of his "impulsive" behavior in visiting prostitutes. The reality is that he paid months in advance (committing himself to seeing prostitutes rather than committing himself to avoiding them) and in one case flew a prostitute from Washington D.C. to New York – managing to violate Federal as well as State law in the process. Similarly, when Rush Limbaugh was discovered to be carrying large quantities of Viagra from the Dominican Republic it was widely suspected that he had gone there on a "sex vacation" – hardly something done impulsively at the last minute. Or perhaps a case more familiar to most of us – the Las Vegas102 vacation? This is planned well in advance and we spend months enjoying the anticipation of the rush of engaging in impulsive behavior. Of course, the more sensible among us may plan to limit the amount of cash we bring along.

The point here is simple: our "rational" self is not intrinsically in conflict with our impulsive self. The evidence is that our rational self often facilitates rather than overrides the activities of our impulsive self.

## Procrastination

Prominent on Akerlof's list of "behavioral" phenomena is procrastination. This is something we are all familiar with – but what is it exactly? When I quizzed a behavioral economist for examples he came up with the following list.

- Paying taxes the day before the deadline

- Christmas shopping on Christmas eve
- Buying party supplies for something like a New Years Eve party or a 4th of July party at the last minute
- Buying Halloween costumes at the last minute
- Delaying the purchase of concert tickets
- Waiting to buy plane tickets for Thanksgiving

Here is the thing: none of these is the least irrational. In each case an unpleasant task is delayed until the deadline. But if the task is unpleasant and we are impatient – as economists assume we are – then the best thing to do is to wait until the deadline. In the folk story:

> The king had a favorite horse that he loved very much. It was a beautiful and very smart stallion, and the king had taught it all kinds of tricks. The king would ride the horse almost every day, and frequently parade it and show off its tricks to his guards.
>
> A prisoner who was scheduled to be executed soon saw the king with his horse through his cell window and decided to send the king a message. The message said, "Your Royal Highness, if you will spare my life, and let me spend an hour each day with your favorite horse for a year, I will teach your horse to sing."
>
> The king was amused by the offer and granted the request. So, each day the prisoner would be taken from his cell to the horse's paddock, and he would sing to the horse "La-la-la-la" and would feed the horse sugar and carrots and oats, and the horse would neigh. And, all the guards would laugh at him for being so foolish.
>
> One day, one of the guards, who had become somewhat friendly with the prisoner, asked him, "Why do you do such a foolish thing every day singing to the horse, and letting everyone laugh at you? You know you can't teach a horse to sing. The year will pass, the horse will not sing, and the king will execute you."
>
> The prisoner replied, "A year is a long time. Anything can happen. In a year the king may die. Or I may die. Or the horse may die. Or... The horse may learn to sing."

The focus on procrastination is behavioral economics at its worst. Here a phenomenon that for the most part is rational and sensible is promoted to a glaring contradiction of standard theory that requires an elaborate psychological explanation. It is true in some of the examples above that there might be a cost of delaying: tickets might sell out before the deadline and so forth. However that simply introduces a trade-off between buying early and closer to the deadline, and different rational people with different degrees of patience, and who value the tickets differently may well choose to behave differently, some procrastinating and some not.

We previously discussed the DellaVigna and Malmendier [2006] study of health club memberships. They provide evidence that people pay extra to self-commit to exercising. They also discuss procrastination: the fact that people after they stop attending delay canceling their memberships. Unlike the example above there is no issue of delaying an unpleasant task until a deadline. So: is this the irrational procrastination Akerlof is concerned about? DellaVigna and Malmendier's data shows that people typically procrastinate for an average of 2.3 months before canceling their self-renewing membership. The average amount lost is nearly $70 against canceling at the first moment that attendance stops.

Leaving aside the fact that it may take a while after last attending to make the final decision to quit the club, we are all familiar with this kind of procrastination. Why cancel today when we could cancel tomorrow instead? Or given the monthly nature of the charge, why not wait until next month. One behavioral interpretation of procrastination is that people are *naïve* in the sense that they do not understand that they are procrastinators. That is, they put off until tomorrow, believing they will act tomorrow, and do not understand that tomorrow they will face the same problem and put off again. There may indeed be some people that behave this way. But if we grant that people who put off cancellation are making a mistake, there are several kinds of untrue beliefs they might hold. One is that they falsely believe that they are not procrastinators. DellaVigna and Malmendier assert that canceling a membership is a simple inexpensive procedure. Supposing this to be true, it might be that people falsely believe that it will be a time consuming hassle. Foolishly they think canceling will involve endless telephone menus, employees who vanish in back rooms for long periods of time, and all the other things we are familiar with whenever we try to cancel an automatic credit card charge.

The question to raise about the "naïve" interpretation is this. Which is more likely: that people are misinformed about something they have observed every day for their entire lives (whether or not they are procrastinators) or something that they have observed infrequently and for which the data indicates costs may be high (canceling)? Learning theory suggests the latter – people are more likely to make mistakes about things they know little about. Behavioral economics argue the former is more likely.

# Risk Preferences: the Allais Paradox

Uncertainty surrounds us, and is central to modern economic models. People's attitude towards risk and uncertainty is at the core of economic theory. Although behavioral economists sling around terms such as "loss aversion" to explain that the standard model is deficient deviations from the theory are in fact quite subtle, and indeed, impossible to understand without knowing something about the standard theory.

The basic economic theory of choice under uncertainty is called *expected utility* theory – the theory dates back to Daniel Bernoulli in 1738. However: utility theory is a construct. What is always fundamental in economics are preferences – in this case preferences between different risky prospects or lotteries.

For concreteness, suppose that there are four possible outcomes of equal probability. For example we might put four numbers in a hat and pull one out at random. Or we might flip two coins – this also leads to four equally probable outcomes: both coins heads, both tails, the first heads the second tails, and vice versa. One lottery might assign a certain amount of one dollar to each outcome. Another might assign a loss of two dollars to the first outcome and a gain of two dollars to the other three outcomes. Which would you choose? Or more relevant – does your choice depend on whether the outcome is determined by flipping two coins or drawing one of four numbers from a hat? Economists suspect it does not, and if it does not they say that your preferences satisfy the *reduction of compound lotteries axiom*. We also imagine that if you prefer lottery A to lottery B and B to C, then you prefer lottery A to C. This is called *transitivity*.

Now look at the table below with three equally likely outcomes

|  | *Outcome 1* | *Outcome 2* | *Outcome 3* |
|---|---|---|---|
| *Lottery 1* | 1 | $x$ | 3 |
| *Lottery 2* | 2 | $x$ | 2 |

Lottery Winnings

This describes the amount of money you get paid based on the outcome, or more accurately it describes many different possible lotteries, depending on the amount $x$ you get if outcome 2 occurs. Do you prefer Lottery 1 or Lottery 2? Does it depend on $x$? Economists imagine that $x$ doesn't really matter to most people since you get the same $x$ in outcome 2 in both lotteries.

So really the choice is between 1 in Outcome 1 with 3 in Outcome 3 versus 2 in both outcomes. If you prefer lottery 2 for $x = 2$ then we suspect you will prefer it when $x = 5$ or some other number. This is called the *independence of irrelevant alternatives* or just the *independence axiom*: the result of Outcome 2 is irrelevant as you get the same amount in both lotteries.

Finally, suppose that given three outcomes A, B and C, where A is better than B is better than C, we can find some probabilities between A and C that would leave you indifferent to B. That is, since B is in between A and C in your ranking, if you had a low enough probability of A and high enough probability of C, you should be willing to take that in place of B and vice versa. This is called the *continuity axiom*.

If your lottery preferences satisfy all of these axioms: reduction of compound lotteries, transitivity, independence and continuity, then it is possible to give a mathematical description of your preferences by means of a utility function – often called the Von-Neumann Morgenstern utility function[4] – that assigns utility numbers to outcomes and in which you rank lotteries by the expected value – the probability weighted average – of those utility numbers. That in brief is expected utility theory.

Most people find the axioms relatively plausible – few argue that they wish to behave otherwise: for example that there are lotteries A better than B better than C, but really C is better than A. Or that they would reverse their choices based on irrelevant alternatives. Unfortunately, when given real (or hypothetical) choices, people do violate the axioms. This was first pointed out by the economist Maurice Allais in 1953.

In the original version of the Allais paradox you are offered a (hypothetical for obvious reasons) choice between getting $1 million for sure versus a risky choice giving $1 million with 89% probability, $5 million with 10% probability and nothing with 1% probability. Most people choose the $1 million for sure. You are then offered an alternative scenario in which you choose between an 11% chance of $1 million (and 89% of nothing); or a 10% chance of $5 million. Most people prefer the 10% chance of $5 million. Unluckily the only difference between the two scenarios lies in an irrelevant alternative: in the first scenario there are 89 cases where you get $1 million in both lotteries and the second scenario differs only in that in those same 89 cases you get nothing. Therefore, if you choose the sure thing in Scenario 1 and the $5 million in Scenario 2, you have violated the independence axiom.

---

4   Their 1944 book systematically developed the theory first proposed by Bernoulli.

I don't know if this example will work for you but give it a shot. I give this to my undergraduate students in class, and it worked well for years. Then one year – the year that all the students said that their life ambition was to become rich by selling commercial real estate – it stopped working because nobody chose the $1 million for sure in the first scenario. What I did was to – understanding that $1 million isn't worth what it was in 1953, especially not to a group of people hoping to earn much more than that – change the millions to billions and all was well. Thus, if the numbers above don't work for you, try it again with billions.

There are a number of possible explanations of the Allais paradox examined over the years by economists. Rubinstein [1988] and Leland [1994] suggest people might focus on the fact that a 1% chance of getting nothing is quite different than a 0% chance, but be less cognizant of the difference between 89% and 90%, while Andreoni and Sprenger [2010] presume that people perceive the probabilities zero and one quite differently than other probabilities. Machina [1982] suggests a systematic non-linearity of preference in probabilities. Behavioral economists and psychologists have their own theory – prospect theory – that we will come to shortly.

## Risk Preferences: the Rabin Paradox

The Allais paradox is not widely viewed as an important deviation from the theory of expected utility by economists. The reason is that to get the paradox the numbers in the gambles must be very carefully chosen. As I mentioned, with my undergraduates the paradox vanished one day because the value of a million fell enough that they decided that it was worth giving up a sure million for a 10% chance at $5 million and an 89% chance of the $1 million despite the 1% risk of getting nothing. If we don't craft the numbers just right, we don't get a reversal. Typical economic choices don't involve such carefully chosen numbers, so the paradox does not have much practical import.

A much more significant puzzle is that raised by Matthew Rabin in *Econometrica* in 2000. To explain that puzzle we must examine the most important application of expected utility theory – the idea of risk aversion. There are few terms more misused than this one – even by economists who should know better. People say "I don't buy tickets in the state lottery because I am risk averse." As it happens for every dollar you bet in the state lottery you will win on average about 50 cents.[5] That isn't risk aversion. Risk aversion means that if for every dollar you bet in the state lottery you will win on average more than one dollar, you still don't bet because of the risk of losing. For example, I hold up a $100 bill and a $10 bill and offer to flip a coin: if it is heads you get the $110; if you lose you give me $100. If you say no, then you are risk averse. This is because the expected value of a 50% chance of $110 and a 50% chance of -$100 is five dollars. If a gamble has a positive expected value and you reject it you are risk averse. By contrast, if it has a negative expected value and you accept it you are risk loving. So in the case of the state lottery, we can say that someone who purchases tickets is risk loving, but we can't say whether or not someone who doesn't purchase tickets is risk loving or risk averse.

Turning back to the win $110 lose $100 with equal chance, if you are just on the margin between accepting and rejecting the bet, then we say you have a *risk premium* of $5 because you are willing to give up an expected gain of that amount to avoid the uncertainty of the gamble. Economists have a measure of how risk averse people are called the *coefficient of relative risk aversion*. Exactly what this is can be a bit complicated to explain, but the key idea is this: let us measure the stakes by the proportion of your lifetime wealth. For example if you are worth a million dollars, then a loss of $100,000 represents a 10% loss. The key feature of the coefficient of relative risk aversion is that if my coefficient is twice your coefficient, then for any given gamble, I will demand twice the risk premium you do. If we have the same wealth, and your risk premium is $5 for the win $110 lose $100 with equal probability, then my risk premium is $10, meaning in addition to foregoing the gamble and giving up $5, I'd be willing to pay an extra $5 to avoid it.

With these tools under our belt, let me give my own version of the Rabin paradox – drawn from years of watching experimental papers presented in which coefficients of relative risk were measured – and in which the presenters never once mentioning that the results are nonsense by three orders of magnitude. Suppose that your lifetime wealth is $860,000 which is about the median in the United States. Suppose also that you are indifferent between a 70%:30% chance of $40 and $32 and the same chances of $77 and $2 – which many people are in the laboratory (Holt and Laury [2002]). Then your coefficient of relative risk aversion is 27,950. If this sounds like a big number, it is. One important puzzle much studied

---

5    See for example Garrett and Sobel [1999].

by economists is why the rate of return on stocks is so much higher than on bonds, given that stocks are not all that much riskier. One thing we can do is to calculate how risk averse a person would be who is on the margin between buying stocks (an S&P 500 index mutual fund) and U.S. government bonds – a situation many of us are in. The answer is that the corresponding coefficient of relative risk aversion is 8.84. This is over three orders of magnitude different than the answer we find in the laboratory.

This enormously higher risk aversion for small stakes gambles than for large stakes gambles was documented in a clever way by Matt Rabin. It poses an enormous challenge for economics and one that by and large economists have not attempted to address. It flavors laboratory research, which sometimes take as given the relatively low risk aversion observed for large stakes gambles and proceeds to ignore the fact that we know that for the small stakes gambles we observe in the laboratory people are far more risk averse. It poses also a difficult theoretical challenge since the existing theory of expected utility is not able to explain this enormous discrepancy. While several explanations have been offered, none has achieved widespread acceptance. The most widely used theory that can potentially explain the discrepancy is the psychological theory called *prospect theory* – which however is not widely used by economists.

## Risk Preferences: Prospect Theory to the Rescue?

Because of the Allais and Rabin paradoxes psychologists widely regard the expected utility theory used by economists as nuts. As mentioned they also have a serious alternative called prospect theory. Prospect theory differs from expected utility theory in two ways. First, it allows for what is called a *probability distortion*. This says that people tend to exaggerate low probabilities. Second, it incorporates what is called a *reference point*. This says that people are not concerned with the effect of a gamble on some sort of measure of overall well-being, but rather with the gains and losses relative to a reference point. If I seem vague about what the reference point is there is a reason: it is treated as an unknown value that varies from setting to setting in an unexplained manner. From the perspective of an economist this is a bug that renders the theory unusable. A theory that says behavior depends on some unknown variable that changes in an unexplained way does not make very useful predictions.

Let us start with the part of prospect theory that says that people over-weight low probabilities and under-weight high probabilities. Is this true? Bruhin, Fehr-Duda and Epper [2007] (economists, by the way) carry out a careful experimental study to find what the probability weighting function might be. Suppose that $P_i$ is the chance of winning one of two prizes $x_i \geq 0$, where $i$ is the generic name for prize 1 and prize 2. For the mathematically inclined – and if you think you can do behavioral economics without mathematics, think again – they find that for many people if we define a utility function over the probability and prizes by the formula

$$U = \Sigma_i \frac{.846\, P_i}{.846P_i^{.414} + (1-Pi)^{.414}}\, x_i^{1.056}$$

then the gambling behavior of these people is described by picking the gamble that yields the highest numerical value of the utility.

One issue with theories, however, is that they make a range of predictions – not only in the laboratory, but also outside the laboratory. Which would you rather have?

A.   $5,000 for sure (or)
B.   a 50–50 coin-flip between $9,700 dollars and nothing

People I have asked all prefer alternative A. However the utility function above yields a higher numerical value for option B, thus according to Bruhin, Fehr-Duda, and Epper, such an individual will choose B. As the "typical" person doesn't do this, prospect theory is not without its own paradoxes.

To pursue this further, prospect theory is motivated in part by the Allais paradox. Recall that there are two scenarios: in Scenario 1 you choose between a certain $1 million and a lottery offering a nothing with a 1% probability, $1 million with an 89% probability, and $5 million with a 10% probability. Most people choose the certain $1 million. In Scenario 2 you are offered the choice between two lotteries. The first lottery offers nothing with 89% probability and $1 million with 11% probability, while the second offers nothing with 90% probability and $5 million with 10% probability. Here most people choose the 10% chance of $5 million. Prospect theory offers a possible resolution of this paradox because smaller probabilities are exaggerated, making the first choice relatively unattractive in Scenario 1, but not so much so in Scenario 2. Unfortunately the Bruhin, Fehr-Duda and Epper [2007] utility function above while explaining the laboratory data also predicts that the "typical" person will not exhibit the Allais paradox.

Prospect theory is largely an empirical and experimental based theory. Many of the experiments on which it is based are for hypothetical money or for very small amounts of money. A question that is always important in this context – the more so given the Rabin paradox – is how the laboratory results reflect on real behavior. Indeed, it turns out that the empirical research underlying prospect theory is a case study in how problematic this can be. One of the main hypotheses in prospect theory is that people are risk averse for gains, but risk loving for losses. However: it isn't all that easy to present people with the possibility of losses in the laboratory. We can't easily force people to engage in gambles that involve them losing money. If we start them off with an initial stake that they can lose, we have to worry about the impact that stake has on their "reference point." As a result experiments involving gains have typically been done for larger stakes than experiments involving losses and indeed most of the losses have been hypothetical rather than real. That raises the possibility that people aren't risk averse for gains and risk loving for losses at all, but rather that they are risk loving for small (real) stakes and risk averse for (real) large stakes – quite different than is assumed in prospect theory.

In 2006 two clever investigators, Bosch-Domenech and Silvestre examined the possibility that risk aversion and risk loving are driven by the stakes rather than by gains and losses. To allow the possibility of substantial losses, they endowed subjects with money in one experiment, then – to avoid any possible effect of having given them money – they conducted the gambles in a second experiment several months later. What they found is that prospect theory is wrong: risk aversion and risk loving are in fact driven by stakes and not by losses and gains.

Interestingly there is evidence outside the laboratory that people are risk loving with respect to losses. For example: in the recent crisis, and historically as well, bankers have always appeared to be willing to gamble a small probability of a large loss for a modest increase in the average return. Prospect theory appears to predict this kind of behavior, and indeed we find Godlewski in 2007 proposing exactly this possibility. There are two problems with this analysis. First, as we just pointed out, laboratory data does not show that people are risk loving for substantial losses. Second, standard expected utility theory predicts that bankers should gamble on losses.

Have you heard of the "hail Mary pass" in football? That's when a team just throws the ball wildly down the field gambling that somehow they will get lucky and someone on their team will grab it and score. Usually the opposite happens, the other team grabs it and scores instead. Of course the reason teams do this is because the game is ending, they are behind, and it is unlikely that they will win the game. Losing the game by 13 points rather than 6 doesn't matter, and the only way they can hope to win is by gambling. Bankers face a similar situation – not that their game is about to end, but rather that their loss is truncated. If they win, they get to pocket a nice commission. If they lose – then the government steps in and bails them out. When bigger losses don't matter – either because it doesn't matter how much you lose the game by or because the government will bail you out no matter how great the loss – expected utility theory – and common sense – indicate that gambling is a good idea.

This notion that prospect theory is somehow needed to explain the gambling behavior of bankers is once again behavioral economics at its worst. Expected utility theory provides a simple and obvious explanation for what we see. Prospect theory is not needed here.

In summary, expected utility theory has its paradoxes. Prospect theory is an effort to explain those paradoxes. Unfortunately when subject to the same scrutiny as expected utility theory it has its own equally serious paradoxes.

To give credit to psychologists – the fact that prospect theory allows attitudes towards risk to depend on the context (or a reference point) at least attempts to come to grips with the Rabin paradox. I do not know of any way to explain the wildly different attitudes towards large and small risks without some model of context dependence. Unfortunately the lack of an adequate theory of the reference point renders prospect theory useless for economists.[6]

## Risk Preferences: How Research in Economics Works

Critics of economic theory seem to be under the impression that economists are wedded to elegant models and oblivious to any facts that might fly in the face of those models. Nothing could be less true. A case study involving a famous and important paradox helps to illustrate the point.

---

6    Plott in his 1996 review of one of Kahneman's many attacks on standard economics carefully examines why his proposed theory is useless for economists.

In 1981 Shiller gathered over 100 years of data on stock market returns, bond returns, and consumption data. He observed that under rational expectations the price of stocks is supposed to be a weighted average of future dividend payments. For any fixed weights this implies that prices should fluctuate less than dividends: something that is not true in the data. Unfortunately for this calculation – the so called *excess volatility puzzle* – this is only true for fixed weights, and theory and evidence suggests that the weights fluctuate enough to cause the observed fluctuations in prices. Several years later in 1985 Mehra and Prescott pointed out a rather more serious puzzle in Shiller's data, the *equity premium puzzle.*

If we look at the returns in Shiller's data, properly adjusted for inflation, we find that safe government bonds had a return of about 1.9%, while stocks had a much higher return of 7.5%.[7] This of course isn't much of a puzzle: it is much easier to lose your shirt by investing in stocks than in bonds, as many investors recently have had the misfortunate to verify. In fact, we can measure relatively well the amount of risk involved in stock investment: in the Shiller data a measure of the risk is the standard error of the stock return, which is 18.1%. This means that roughly 68% of the time stock returns lie between 7.5% − 18.1% = −10.6% and 7.5% + 18.1% = 25.6%. That seems pretty risky, but when we apply our tool of relative risk aversion to ask how risk averse an individual would have to be to be indifferent between investing in stocks and bonds, we find that it should be around 8.84, which is the result we reported before in our discussion of the Rabin paradox. That number is pretty small compared to the laboratory value of 27,950, but never-the-less it turns out to be too large.

What can we mean by too large? After all, people are how risk averse they are. Perhaps their risk aversion is indeed 8.84. However, the coefficient of risk aversion governs behavior in a number of domains, so it may be that their behavior in other domains is inconsistent with 8.84 for stocks and bonds. And indeed there are two major problems with this number. First, as pointed out by Boldrin and Levine [2001], any coefficient of relative risk aversion bigger than one implies that the stock market prices respond to bad news by going up – the opposite of what we observe. Second, as observed by Mehra and Prescott, in standard theory the coefficient of relative risk aversion determines our willingness to save. In particular in the same Shiller data

---

7    Stock returns are measured by returns on the Standard and Poor's 500 index. This is the broadest measure of stock returns that is available over such a long period of time.

used to compute stock and bond returns, real per capita consumption in the United States grew on average 1.8% per year. It turns out that an individual with a coefficient of relative risk aversion of 8.84 faced with a 1.9% return on bonds would not wish their consumption to grow nearly this fast: they would wish to borrow heavily against the future. It is this contradiction between the amount of risk aversion observed in choosing between stocks and bonds and savings behavior that is the equity premium puzzle.

So what have economists done in response to this puzzle? Built ever more elegant and less relevant models? They can't easily be accused of ignoring it: a citation count on Google Scholar[8] shows 3,726 follow-on papers to Mehra and Prescott. Many of these papers were published in top journals such as the *Journal of Political Economy,* the *American Economic Review* and *Econometrica.* Did anyone turn to prospect theory? Of course that was tried – and discarded along with various other approaches for a very simple reason – because it didn't help explain the puzzle. One can fairly easily find various papers by "behavioral economists" claiming that the puzzle was solved by various means including prospect theory, however what these papers have in common is that they don't recognize that the puzzle involves not the fact that people are very risk averse, but rather that their risk aversion in the stock/bond decision contradicts their behavior in other domains.

What is striking about this is that prospect theory appears to have at its core an idea that might help explain the equity premium puzzled: the idea of a reference point that leads to different behavior in different domains. Unfortunately prospect theory's reference point doesn't say anything about the stock/bond domain versus the savings domain. In 1990, fortunately, Constantinides (an economist) produced a model of habit formation that not only provided a reference point governing risk behavior and intertemporal behavior, but provided a clear theory of what determined the reference point. The idea is a simple and intuitive one: as we consume at a particular level it becomes a habit, and as the novelty wears off, we need increases in consumption to feed our utility. Conversely, declines in consumption are very difficult to bear, having habituated ourselves to a higher level. This makes us very risk averse. At the same time it causes us to demand ever growing consumption as we race to get ahead of our habit.

One question – rarely asked by behavioral economists – is whether such a substantial change in assumptions about individual behavior might – while

---

8    Search conducted October 23, 2011 at 3:32 AM Pacific Standard Time.

explaining one thing, namely the equity premium – also unexplain other things. For example, we can explain around 50% of business cycle fluctuations using a straightforward model of growth – without habit formation. Naturally economists have examined whether the habit formation model has unpleasant as well as pleasant implications. One reason the model has become popular is because in 2001 Boldrin, Christiano and Fisher showed that introducing habit formation into a real business cycle model if anything improves its ability to explain economic fluctuations.

It is worth mentioning also a related class of models called *consumption lock-in* models. These models are technically a bit different than habit formation models but have a very similar flavor: they assume that after you choose a particular level of consumption it is costly to adjust it right away, either up or down. These models also date back to 1990 when they were introduced by Grossman and Laroque. As Grossman and Laroque argued, while standard theory says that people ought to adjust their consumption in response to changes in stock market prices, nobody is terribly likely to sell their house and buy a slightly larger or smaller one in response to a modest change in stock prices (although they might skimp a bit on maintenance if prices fall).

In 2001 Gabaix and Laibson produced a very simple version of the consumption lock-in model showing that a lock-in of about a year and a half is what is needed to explain the equity premium. One advantage of these models over habit formation is that when combined with a model of self-control they can also produce the Rabin paradox: this was shown by Fudenberg and Levine in 2006.

The key thing to note is that these models were a response to a real problem that concerned economists. None of them are "behavioral" in the sense of Akerlof or Ariely, and indeed, nobody has come yet up with a sensible explanation of asset prices based on irrationality. Moreover: there is no shortage of explanations of the equity premium – explanations ranging from taxes to problems with the way the data were chosen have been proposed. Our problem is a surfeit of riches: we have too many explanations of the equity premium puzzle, not too few.

# 8. Learning and Friends

*Nash equilibrium describes a situation in which players have identical and exactly correct beliefs about the strategies each player will choose. How and when might the players come to have correct beliefs, or at least beliefs that are close enough to being correct that the outcome corresponds to a Nash equilibrium?* Fudenberg and Kreps, 1993

Do economists blindly assume that people are rational and have rational expectations? Ironically the notion of rational expectations that is widely attacked by non-economists as unrealistic is the least obnoxious of the assumptions about beliefs that economists make. The notion that would be attacked if the attackers had any idea what they were talking about is the idea of *common knowledge*. Common knowledge asserts that not only do I know what you are going to do and you know what I am going to do – but that I know that you know what I am going to do, and so forth and so on. To take a somewhat non-economic example, a husband and a wife love each other, and both know that the other loves them, and each knows that the other knows that they are loved and so forth and so on. In the case of a marriage this might indeed be true... but to take a more economic example – can this reasonably be believed to be true of stock traders? Rational expectations theory merely says that we share the same beliefs; common knowledge says that we have a mutual deep understanding of each others' beliefs.

The further irony is that economists have not generally assumed either rational expectations or common knowledge for the last two decades. Rather, in modern theory, these are conclusions rather than assumptions – and conclusions that are only true under certain circumstances.

Game theory entered economics in a big way in the late 1970s and early 1980s. At that time the assumptions of rationality and common knowledge were taken for granted. From the standpoint of a science this is understandable: one walks before running, and there is little point in challenging assumptions before their implications are known. By the late 1980s – long before behavioral economics was in vogue – the inadequacy of the strong rationality assumptions underlying game theory was creating discontent among game theorists. In 1988 two top theorists, Drew Fudenberg and David Kreps, wrote a very influential – although never published – paper examining how equilibrium in games might arise from a process of boundedly rational learning rather than some sort of hyper-rational introspection. The theoretical work that flowered over the next two decades is now very much part of mainstream economics: in addition to economists, computer scientists have been very active in developing theories of learning in games.

I can hardly do justice to the subject of learning in games in a single chapter of a non-technical book. Yet from the perspective of someone who works on learning theory behavioral economics poses a great puzzlement. It talks extensively of biases and errors in decision making. However the great mystery to learning theorists is not why people learn so badly – it is why they learn so well.

Back up for a moment – behavioral economists, psychologists, economists and computer scientists model human learning by what can only be described as naïve and primitive models. Some of these models have various errors and biases built in. Even those models designed by computer scientists to make the best possible decisions cannot come close to the learning ability of the average human child – indeed, it is questionable that these models learn as well as the average chimpanzee or even rat.

The motivation for equilibrium models – and the rational expectations revolution – is simply that if we have to choose between our best models of learning and simply throwing in the towel and assuming that people learn perfectly – for most situations of interest to economists the assumption of perfect learning fits the facts far better than our best models of learning.

This is not to say that learning theory has not contributed to our understanding of economics. A fundamental tenet of learning theory is you can only learn to the extent that you have experience or other data to learn from. In the absence of information there is no reason to imagine that people are unbiased, or do not exhibit "irrational" or "behavioral" modes of decision making. In many ways the idea of incorrect beliefs is fundamental to learning theory – if beliefs were always correct there would be nothing to learn about.

To understand more clearly how learning theory helps us understand real behavior, let's examine the central modification to equilibrium theory that arises from the theory of learning – the notion of *self-confirming equilibrium*.

## Learning and Self-confirming Equilibrium

An important aspect of learning theory is the distinction between active learning and passive learning. We learn passively by observing the consequences of what we do simply by being there. However we cannot learn the consequences of things we do not do, so unless we actively experiment by trying different things, we may remain in ignorance.

In mainstream modern economic theory, a great deal of attention is paid to how players learn their way to "equilibrium" and what kind of equilibrium might result. It has long been recognized that players often have little incentive to experiment with alternative courses of action and may, as a result, get stuck doing less well than they would if they had more information. The concept of *self-confirming equilibrium* from Fudenberg and Levine [1993] captures that idea. It requires that beliefs be correct about the things that players see – but they may have incorrect beliefs about things they do not see.

We can illustrate this idea with the ultimatum bargaining game from Chapter 4. Recall that one player proposes the division of an amount of money – often $10, and usually in increments of 5 cents – and the second player may accept, in which case the money is divided as agreed on, or reject, in which case neither player gets anything. If the second player is selfish, he must accept any offer that gives him more than zero. Given this, the first player should ask for – and get – at least $9.95. That is the reasoning of subgame perfect equilibrium. As we observed the prediction that the first player asks for and gets $9.95 is strongly rejected in the laboratory.

Now let us apply the notion of self-confirming equilibrium to this game. Players know the consequences of the offer they make, but not the consequences of offers that they do not make. Using this concept we can distinguish between knowing losses, representing losses a player might reasonably know about, and unknowing losses that might be due to imperfect learning. We earlier computed (in Chapter 5) that in the Roth et al. [1991] data on average players are losing about $0.99 per game. Of that amount, $0.34 are knowing losses due to second players rejecting offers. The remaining

$0.63 are due to the first mover making demands that are either too great and too likely to be rejected, or too small.[1] Since the first mover only observes the consequences of the demand actually made, any loss due to making a demand that is too high or too low can be unknowing. Given that players only got to play ten times, it is not surprising that first movers did not have a good idea of the likelihood of different offers being accepted and rejected.

Notice that there is an important message here. Between social preferences – a major focus of behavioral economics – and learning – a major focus of mainstream economics – in the ultimatum bargaining experiment the role of learning is relatively more important than social preferences. In addition a reasonable measure of the failure of standard theory is not the $0.99 loss out of $10.00, but rather the $0.34 knowing loss.

## Self-confirming Equilibrium and Economic Policy

The use of self-confirming equilibrium has become common in economics. A simpleexampleadaptedfromSargent,WilliamsandZhao[2006a]byFudenberg and Levine [2009] illustrates the idea and shows how it can be applied to concrete economic problems. Consider a game between a government and a typical or representative consumer. First, the government chooses high or low inflation. Then consumers choose high or low unemployment. Consumers always prefer low unemployment. The government prefers low inflation to high inflation, but cares more about unemployment being low than about inflation. If we apply "full" rationality (subgame perfection), we may reason that the consumer will always choose low unemployment. The government recognizing this will always choose low inflation.

Suppose that the government believes incorrectly that low inflation leads to high unemployment – a belief that was widespread at one time. Since they care more about employment than inflation they will keep inflation high – and by doing so never learn that their beliefs about low inflation are false. This is a simple example of self-confirming equilibrium. Beliefs are correct about those things that are observed – high inflation – but not those that are not observed – low inflation.

Such a simple example cannot possibly do justice to the long history of inflation – for example in the United States. Some information about the consequences of low inflation is generated if only because inflation is accidentally low at times. Sargent, Williams and Zhao [2006a] show how

---

1    The details of these calculations can be found in Fudenberg and Levine [1997].

a sophisticated dynamic model of learning about inflation enables us understand how U.S. Federal Reserve policy evolved post World War II to ultimately result in the conquest of U.S. inflation. More to the point, it also enables us to understand why it took so long – a cautionary note for economic policy makers.

# Self-confirming Equilibrium and Economic Crises

While the current economic crisis is surprising and new to non-economists, it is much less so to economists who have observed and studied similar episodes throughout the world. Here too learning seems to play an important role. Prior to the current crisis Sargent, Williams and Zhao [2006b] examined a series of crises in Latin America from a learning theoretic point of view. They assume that consumers have short-run beliefs that are correct, but have difficulty correctly anticipating long run events (the collapse of a "bubble"). Periodic crises arise as growth that is unsustainable in the long run takes place, but consumers cannot correctly foresee that far into the future.

In talking about the crisis, there is a widespread belief that bankers and economists "got it wrong." Economists anticipate events of this sort, but by their nature their timing is unpredictable. Bankers by way of contrast can hardly be accused of acting less than rationally. Their objective is not to preserve their banks or take care of their customers – it is to line their own pockets. They seem to have taken advantage of the crisis to do that very effectively. If you can pay yourself bonuses during the upswing, and have the government cover your losses on the downswing, there is not much reason to worry about the business cycle.

# The Persistence of Superstition

What could be more irrational than superstition? If people are rational learners, won't they learn that their superstitions are wrong? How can superstition persist in the face of evidence?

In fact no behavioral explanation is needed. Rational learning predicts the persistence of certain kinds of superstition. Take the code of Hammurabi[2] as an example.

> If anyone bring an accusation against a man, and the accused go to the river and leap into the river, if he sink in the river his accuser shall take possession

---

2   The code of Hammurabi consists of 282 laws and was created circa 1750 B.C. It is the earliest known written legal code and was inscribed on stone.

of his house. But if the river prove that the accused is not guilty, and he escape unhurt, then he who had brought the accusation shall be put to death, while he who leaped into the river shall take possession of the house that had belonged to his accuser. (2nd law of Hammurabi)

As Fudenberg and Levine [2006] observe, this is puzzling to modern sensibilities for two reasons. First, it is based on a superstition that we do not believe to be true – we do not believe that the guilty are any more likely to drown than the innocent.[3] Second, if people can be easily persuaded to hold a superstitious belief, why such an elaborate mechanism? Why not simply assert that those who are guilty will be struck dead by lightning?

Consider three different games. In the Hammurabi game the first player, a culprit, has to decide whether or not to commit a crime. He prefers to commit the crime if unpunished, but would not do so if he expects to be punished. If he does commit the crime a second player, a witness, must decide whether or not to correctly identify the culprit. The witness prefers to identify a particular enemy rather than the true culprit. After testifying, the accused objects, and the witness is tossed in the river – and most likely drowns.

In the game without the river, the witness simply identifies someone as the culprit and that person is punished.

Finally, in the lightning game, there is no witness, and the culprit – regardless of whether or not the crime was committed – has a small chance of being struck dead by lightning.

In each of these games a superstition can lead to a decision by the first player not to commit a crime. In the first game, the Hammurabi game, the witness believes that she will drown if she lies and survive if she tells the truth. She is definitely wrong: she will drown in both cases. However her beliefs lead her to tell the truth, and knowing this the culprit sensibly decides not to commit the crime. In the second game, the game without the river, the culprit believes that the witness will tell the truth. He is wrong: without any chance of punishment, the witness will lie and identify her enemy. Because of his wrong belief, however, the culprit will again choose not to commit the crime. In the third game, the lightning game, the culprit believes if he commits a crime he will be struck dead by lightning. He is wrong: he is very unlikely to be struck by lightning regardless of whether he commits a crime. Nevertheless, based on this wrong belief, he again optimally chooses not to commit the crime.

---

3    A behavioralist might argue that if the superstition is believed, the guilty might be less inclined to try to swim, so that the superstition would be self-fulfilling. However, no such explanation is needed

In each case the decision not to commit a crime is supported by a superstitious belief: a belief that is objectively false, a belief that evidence should show is false. What differentiates these games? When and why can superstition survive?

Take the lightning game first. From the perspective of Nash equilibrium, the culprit should know that the probability of being struck dead by lightning doesn't depend on whether a crime is committed, so should commit the crime. From the standpoint of self-confirming equilibrium, however, if the culprit chooses not to commit the crime, his belief that he will be struck dead by lightning is purely hypothetical and is never confronted with evidence. Therefore the superstition is a self-confirming equilibrium, but not Nash.

While self-confirming equilibrium is a reasonable description of short-run behavior, it is an unlikely basis for a social norm. Over time some people will commit crimes for one reason or another, and of course they will not be struck dead by lightning. Hence we should not expect "being struck dead by lightning" to be the basis of criminal justice systems, and indeed, historically it does not seem to be so.

Let's look at the game without the river next. Here it is a Nash equilibrium for the culprit not to commit the crime and the witness to tell the truth. Since the witness is never called upon to testify she is indifferent between telling the truth and lying, so it is "rational" to tell the truth. This equilibrium, while not merely self-confirming, but actually Nash, is no more plausible in the long-run than the lightning equilibrium. If people do occasionally commit crimes, the witness – being in fact called upon to testify – will lie, and eventually the superstition that witnesses tell the truth should die in the face of evidence.

In the game without the river, the superstition is consistent with Nash equilibrium, but not subgame perfection. This is relevant because Fudenberg and Levine [2006] show that when people are patient enough to try crimes to see if they "can get away with it" the kind of equilibrium that results is a sort of hybrid between subgame perfection and self-confirming equilibrium called *subgame confirmed equilibrium*. Basically this says that deviations from a Nash equilibrium into a particular subgame should result in a self-confirming equilibrium.

Let's see how this theory works in the game with the river. Here the culprit is supposed to commit the crime only rarely to "see if he can get away with it." He can't in fact get away with it since the witness will tell the truth, so has no reason to commit the crime except for the purpose of learning. The witness tells the truth because she superstitiously believes she has a better chance of surviving the river if she does so. Since she doesn't lie, she doesn't learn that her belief about the river is wrong.

If the culprit commits crimes occasionally to see if "he can get away with it" why does the witness not lie occasionally to see if "she can get away with it?" Neither one expects to "get away with it" – but contemplates the possibility they might. The reason for experimenting is that if the belief of "not being able to get away with it" is wrong, then you will know that in the future that you can "get away with it." Hence "trying it out to see" is an investment in the possibility of future benefits.

When do we invest in the future? If we are patient and the future rewards are not in the too distant future. For the culprit, the rewards are immediate: if you discover you can get away with murder, you can start on a life of crime straight away. It is different for the witness: we don't expect to be called as a witness in a trial very frequently. Thus the benefit of "trying it out to see" is that at some far distant date in the future when called upon to testify again the witness can again lie. The return to the investment is too distant to be worth the trouble.

The bottom line here is that in the Hammurabi game with the river the superstition is about something that lies "off the equilibrium path." That is to say, the superstition is about something that happens very infrequently when the social norm is adhered to. Hence it is not worth investing to see whether or not the superstition is wrong. According to learning theory superstitions of this type are far more robust than superstitions that we have reason to test every day. As Fudenberg and Levine say "Hammurabi had it exactly right: (our simplified interpretation of) his law uses the greatest amount of superstition consistent with patient rational learning."

## Self-Confirming, Nash Equilibrium and Agreeing to Disagree

Common knowledge can be puzzling even to economists. One particularly puzzling conclusion that (seemingly) derives from common knowledge is the *no-trade theorem*. The no-trade theorem says that in the absence of other reasons to trade, people should not trade merely based on informational differences. That is when you offer to bet that a particular horse will win at the race-track I should refuse the bet on the grounds that the only reason you are willing to make the offer is because you know something I don't know. Put that way it seems pretty absurd.

Here is the thing: as Fudenberg and Levine [2005] point out, even in the absence of such rationality, there shouldn't be trade based purely on informational differences. Learning theory alone gives rise to the no-trade theorem. If we are going to on average lose by trading then some of us must be losers – and eventually we should find that out and stop betting. Even in self-confirming equilibrium there can be no trade.

So: should we conclude that people are irrational because they bet on the ponies? Not necessarily. The theorem gives us two reasons why we may have information based trading. First, people may have some reason to trade. For example, at the race-track some people may simply enjoy betting. They happily lose money – and that money serves as incentive for everyone else to bet based on information differences. Second, there may indeed be a sucker born every minute. Over time they discover they are losers and stop betting, but new suckers arrive to take up the slack.

## Keynes Beauty Contest

If John Maynard Keynes is not a hero to behavioral economists, he should be. Nobody believed more strongly that economics was governed by forces of irrationality than he. Stock markets, in particular, he believed were driven by mysterious animal spirits of investors.

Keynes theory of stock markets can be found in Chapter 12 of his 1936 *General Theory*. His notion was that investors want to buy stocks because they think that other investors like those stocks. He gives as an analogy his *beauty contest* game. In this game players must choose the most beautiful woman from six photographs. Players who pick the most popular face win. This in fact is a rather boring coordination game: every face is a Nash equilibrium. Whether this is really how stock markets work may be doubted: it is true that Keynes made a fortune for King's College Cambridge through his stock market investments. It is equally true that at various times he also lost a fortune, so that if he had stepped down as Bursar at a different time his name would be as infamous there as it is today famous.

Be that as it may, in 1995 Rosemarie Nagel conducted some very influential experiments with a simple variation of Keynes beauty contest. In Nagel's game, the players had to choose a number between 0 and 100. The players getting the closest to half the average value of the choices win. Like Keynes beauty contest, what you want to do in this game depends on what you think average opinion is. For example, if you think that people choose randomly, the average should be 50, so you would win by guessing 25. Unlike Keynes beauty contest, this game has a unique Nash equilibrium: it is pretty easy to see that any average greater than 0 can't be an equilibrium since everyone would want to guess less. So everyone has to guess zero. The graph below is taken from Nagel's paper and the dots show choices the third and fourth time the game was played.

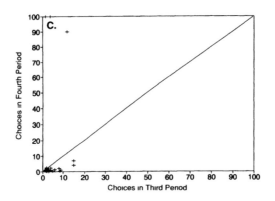

Nagel's Beauty Contest Results

As you can see, the dots are in fact very close to the lower left corner where the theory of Nash equilibrium says they should be.[4]

What is interesting about this experiment is not that we find that experienced players get to Nash equilibrium. What is interesting is that the first time they played they did not get to Nash equilibrium. Nagel's graph reproduced below shows the distribution of choices the first time players played the game.

Not exactly a Nash equilibrium. Since by now we hopefully know not to expect Nash equilibrium in first time play, what is the point? The point is that there is another theory – developed by economists – that does do a good job of explaining what is going on. The idea originates with Nagel, and is further developed by Stahl and Wilson [1994], with recent incarnations in the work of Costa-Gomes, Crawford and Broseta [2001] and Camerer, Ho and Chong [2004]. It has come to be called *level-k theory*.

---

4    I cherry-picked her data: she also reports experiments where you win by guessing 2/3rds the average and 4/3rds the average. These were much less close to a Nash equilibrium – although since people only got to play 4 times, it is hard to regard it as a meaningful violation of the idea that with enough experience players get to equilibrium.

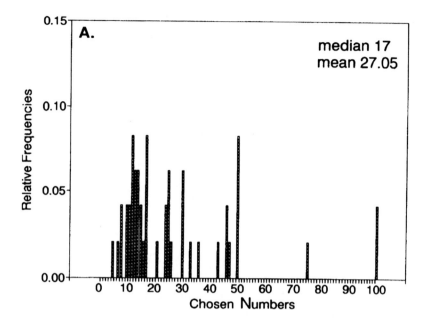

Nagel's Beauty Contest: Results of First Time Play

The idea is relatively simple. People differ in their sophistication. Very naïve individuals – level-0 – play randomly. Less naïve individuals – level-1 – believe that their opponents are of level-0. In general higher level and more sophisticated individuals – level-$k$ – believe that they face a mixture of less sophisticated individuals – people with lower levels of $k$. It turns out that a single common probability belief about the relative likelihood of degrees of sophistication can explain first time play in a variety of experimental games.

While it is impressive that such a simple theory can do a relatively good job of explaining first time play, the idea has yet to gain wide traction in economics. There are likely several reasons for this. First, the types of games in which the theory has been shown to work are relatively simple and unlike the kinds of situations economists are interested in. More to the point, in real markets – stock markets for example – participants are generally relatively experienced, so more likely to exhibit equilibrium behavior than level-$k$ behavior. Still: in modern finance so called "noise traders" who are inexperienced and naïve despite being small in numbers play an important role both in the transmission of information through prices and in price fluctuations. Perhaps level-$k$ theory will ultimately enable us to better model the behavior of these "noisy" individuals.

# Conclusion

Behavioral economics seems to presume that we are most ignorant about the things we are the most familiar with. Despite a lifetime of evidence that we are procrastinators, we stubbornly stick to the belief that we are not. Despite our complete ignorance of the Becker-DeGroot-Marschak elicitation procedure and absence of experience with second price auctions, we comprehend that procedure perfectly, being confused only about how much we are willing to pay for a coffee mug.

Learning theory, by contrast, points the opposite direction. It says that things we are most likely to be mistaken about are the things we know the least about. This is not only common sense, but is supported by overwhelming evidence. If I drop this computer from my lap nobody will argue that it will fly to the ceiling rather than fall to the floor. We have a lifetime of evidence about the law of gravity – and I think we may reasonably say it is common knowledge. I know that you know that I know the law of gravity. By contrast, there is broad disagreement about the possibility and nature of life after death. Some disbelieve in the notion entirely. Others believe in heaven, or hell, or purgatory, or all three. Yet others believe we will be reincarnated as grasshoppers. Of course from a learning theoretic point of view this makes a great deal of sense: if you are reading this book it is unlikely that you are dead, and very few people have come back from the dead to relate their experiences.

# 9. Conclusion: Psychology, Neuroscience and Economics

Economics is commonly condemned for favoring rigor and mathematics over relevance. Perhaps apocryphally the economist Kenneth Boulding is quoted as having said "Mathematics brought rigor to Economics. Unfortunately, it also brought mortis." In 1973 Wassily Leontief in his Nobel Prize lecture – apparently a popular forum for criticizing economics – said

> Page after page of professional economic journals are filled with mathematical formulas leading the reader from sets of more or less plausible but entirely arbitrary assumptions to precisely stated but irrelevant theoretical conclusions.

Much more recently the historian of economic thought, Mark Blaug, said

> Economics was condemned a century ago as "the dismal science," but the dismal science of yesterday was a lot less dismal than the soporific scholasticism of today. To paraphrase the title of a popular British musical: "No Reality, Please. We're Economists." (at http://www.autisme-economie. org/article26.html)

If all these distinguished economists agree, they must be right. And no doubt the solution is behavioral economics!

One version of the solution can be found in a quotation attributed to the dissident economist John Kenneth Galbraith: "In economics it is a far, far wiser thing to be right than to be consistent." Unfortunately this makes little sense: it is hard to see how you can be right in a useful sense by being inconsistent. I can say "the stock market will go up tomorrow." An hour later I can say "the stock market will go down tomorrow." This is certainly inconsistent, and I am bound to be correct (as well as equally bound to be incorrect), but in what respect is it useful? Fortunately if you have read this book, you will have discovered that economics is concerned not with rigor over relevance, but with rigorous relevance, which is an altogether different matter. Economics does not need saving.

If economics does not need saving, it can certainly use improving. Unfortunately behavioral economics does not seem at all focused on the weaknesses of economics. It is true that people have an emotional irrational side that is not well captured by mainstream economic models. By way of contrast, psychologists have long been fascinated with this side of humankind, and have many models and ideas on the subject. In this sense it is perhaps not surprising that much of behavioral economics attempts to import the ideas and models developed by psychologists.

Unfortunately psychology is no more perfect than economics. There is evidence, for example, that pigeons are more intelligent than psychologists. In the 1950s psychologists conducted choice experiments with lights that could flash one of two colors. The goal of the subjects was to guess what light would flash next. If the colors are chosen independently the best thing to do is to guess the most likely color all of the time. Subjects did not do this: they tended to guess each color roughly in proportion to the frequency of the color – for example if the light flashed green 2/3rds the time, they would guess green about 2/3rds of the time. This "failure to optimize" was called *probability matching*. It has been replicated with pigeons as well, for example by Graf, Bullock and Bitterman [1964]. Here is the thing. In 1971 Fiorini went back and examined the data. He found that the light flashes were not independent. If a light flashed green, then the next flash was more likely to be green than red. That means that the best thing to do is to guess whatever color you saw last – resulting in choices roughly proportional to the frequencies of the different color lights. In other words: the pigeons computed the optimum correctly – the psychologists who were studying them did not.

Interestingly these probability matching experiments are the basis of the psychological theory of learning called *reinforcement learning*. That reinforcement learning results in probability matching behavior was pointed out by two economists Borgers and Sarin [2000].

We can make endless jokes about who is smarter: economists, psychologists or pigeons. The point is that both economists and psychologists make mistakes – and both disciplines learn from their mistakes. Psychologists today no more subscribe to probability matching as a theory than economists subscribe to the idea that burying money in the ground is a cure for recessions.

More to the point – it is crucial to recognize that the goals of psychologists and economists are different, and that this has implications for importing ideas from psychology into economics.

The key difference between psychologists and economists is that psychologists are interested in individual behavior while economists are interested in explaining the results of groups of people interacting. Psychologists also are focused on human dysfunction – much of the goal of psychology (the bulk of psychologists are in clinical practices) is to help people become more functional. In fact, most people are quite functional most of the time. Hence the focus of economists on people who are "rational." Certain kinds of events – panics, for example – that are of interest to economists no doubt can benefit from understanding human dysfunctionality. But the balancing of portfolios by mutual fund managers, for example, is not such an obvious candidate. Indeed one of the themes of this book is that in the experimental lab the simplest model of human behavior – selfish rationality with imperfect learning – does an outstanding job of explaining the bulk of the type of behavior that economists are interested in.

Another science that is changing the way we think about decision making is neuroscience. With modern technology such as the fMRI scanner it is now possible to study what happens physically in the brain while decisions are made. As Camerer, Lowenstein and Prelec said in the *Journal of Economic Literature* in 2005.

> This "rational choice" approach has been enormously successful. But now advance in genetics and brain imaging (and other techniques) have made it possible to observe detailed processes in the brain better than every before. Brain scanning [...] shows which parts of the brain are active when people make economic decision. This means that we will eventually be able to replace the simple mathematical ideas that have been used in economics with more neurally-detailed descriptions.

Or as Aldo Rustichini said in 2003

> This new approach, which I consider a revolution should provide a theory of how people decide in economic and strategic situations.[1]

So will peering into the brain revolutionize economics? Almost certainly not. First, when we ask what the revolution is to be, we find from Camerer, Lowenstein and Prelec (for example) that

---

1    Quoted in Blakeslee [2003].

Much aversion to risks is driven by immediate fear responses, which are largely traceable to a small area of the brain called the amygdala. The amygdala is an "internal hypochondriac" which provides "quick and dirty" emotional signals in response to potential fears. But the amygdala also receives cortical inputs which can moderate or override its responses.

Unfortunately, as Gul and Pesendorfer [2005] point out in some detail – economists have no interest in what happens in the amygdala. Worse: not only to we not care what happens in the amygdala, for the kind of decisions we are interested in much of the action does not take place in the brain, nor is it subject to memory and other limitations. Even before we all had personal computers, we had pieces of paper that could be used not only for keeping track of information – but for making calculations as well. For most decisions of interest to economists these external helpers play a critical role – and no doubt lead to a higher level of rationality in decision making than if we had to make all decisions on the fly in our heads.

That is merely the tip of the iceberg. The human brain is a general purpose computing device – with external support it is what computer scientists call a Turing machine. And it is a theorem in computer science that all Turing machines are capable of exactly the same computations. That is – any decision algorithm that is possible we can carry out. We will have as much success understanding decision making by peering into the brain as we will in understanding how Microsoft Word works by peering into a computer chip.

This is not to say that neuroscience will add nothing to economics. If it is not going to replace existing theory or create a revolution, it may be potentially useful. While economic theories are not intended to predict what will happen in the amygdala they may nevertheless be successful at doing so. Insofar as they are, we have an additional way of measuring preferences. Much of "neuroeconomic" research focuses on decisions taken under uncertainty: for example, Glimcher [2002] or Dickhaut et al. [2003]. While trying to understand the decision making process by peering into the brain is useless, our understanding of preferences may be enhanced through brain studies. This is true not only for risk preferences – for example research such as that of Padoa-Schioppa and Assad [2006] show how neurons encode economic values. It must be, after all, that at some level our preferences are biologically determined – if neuroeconomics can help us better measure or understand those preferences it will have indeed helped to improve economics.

Both psychology and neuroscience are focused on individual behavior. Economics is focused on group behavior. This difference is crucial in many ways. There is a small segment of the psychology literature that effectively commits a fallacy of composition, reasoning that if we can explain individual behavior, then this carries over immediately to the group. The most obvious example of this is the idea that if we could somehow make people better – more altruistic, say – then society at large would be better off. This is far from the case – as we discussed earlier, a nice example of an interactive setting where better people result in an inferior society can be found in Hwang and Bowles [2008].

There is a more intuitive way of making this point. From the perspective of his psychiatrist helping Tony Soprano become more functional is a good thing. From a social point of view if this enables him to be a more functional criminal it is a bad thing. Medical ethics are entirely focused on the patient, with no allowance for the role of the patient in society. The bottom line is that what is good for the individual is not always good for society, and we need to use game-theoretic and related models in order to understand the consequences of individual behavior for the entire group.

The need to study groups of potentially large numbers of people – as I write this we are approaching seven billion – imposes constraints on economic models of individual decision making that are not present for psychologists. Economists need simple and broad models of behavior. Narrow complex models of behavior – neurally-detailed descriptions, for example – cannot easily be used to study the behavior of many people interacting. Hence the focus by economists on axiomatic models that provide a reasonable description of particular data while also giving decent results over a broad range of social settings. To take an example, research in psychology on hyperbolic discounting focuses on finding clever functional forms that will fit a broad range of data on human (and animal) behavior involving delayed rewards. From an economist's perspective, such models can be useful in testing and calibrating our own models – but they cannot be usefully embedded in complex social situations.

Another main theme of this book is that behavioral economics can contribute to strengthening existing economic theory, but, at least in its current incarnation, offers no realistic prospect of replacing it. Certain types of "behavioral" models are already important in mainstream economics: these include models of learning; of habit formation; and of the related phenomenon of consumer lock-in. Behavioral criticisms that ignore the great increase in the scope and accuracy of mainstream theory brought about by these innovations miss the mark entirely.

In the other direction are what I would describe as not part of mainstream economics, but rather works in progress that may one day become part of mainstream economics. The idea of level-$k$ thinking is one such. Another that I did not discuss is the idea of ambiguity aversion. This captures the fascination economists have had since Frank Knight's 1921 work with distinguishing mere risk from uncertainty. It is connected as well to the instrumental notion that some of the people we interact with may be dishonest.

The subtitle of this book is "The Ordinary and the Extraordinary" the idea being of course that rationality is the ordinary and irrationality the extraordinary. Mainstream economics focuses on the essential rationality of most people faced with familiar circumstances. Behavioral economics focuses on the irrationality of a few people or with people faced with extraordinary circumstances. Given time economists expect that these same people will rationally adjust their behavior to account for new understandings of reality and not simply repeat the same mistakes over and over again.

If we accept learning as a real phenomenon – we may never the less wonder how long it takes and whether it is really relevant. As John Maynard Keynes famously said "In the long run we are all dead." In laboratory studies a situation may need to be repeated 10, 50 or even 500 times before an equilibrium is reached. What does that translate to outside the laboratory? Would it take years to reach an equilibrium? Decades? In practice the adjustment can be astoundingly fast. A dramatic example took place on September 11, 2001.

In the 1990s there were around 18 aircraft hijackings a year. Most ended peacefully and the longer a hijacking persisted the more often there was a peaceful ending. Rationally flight crews were trained in the FAA-approved "Common Strategy." Hijackers' demands should be complied with, the plane should be landed safely as soon as possible, and security forces should be allowed to handle the situation. Passengers should sit quietly, and nobody should play "hero." This advice was well-established, rational, successful, and strongly validated by decades of experience.

Things changed abruptly on September 11, 2001 when hijackers, rather than landing planes and making demands, used the hijacked aircraft for suicide attacks on ground targets. The rational response was no longer the passive "Common Strategy" but rather to resist at any cost. Indeed since

September 11, 2001 passengers and flight crews – who rarely resisted prior to that time – have equally rarely failed to resist.

How long did it take to overturn the long-established and successful "Common Rule?" The timeline is instructive. At 8:42 a.m. on September 11, 2001, United Airlines Flight 93 took off. The first evidence of a regime change occurred four minutes later when American Airlines Flight 11 crashed into the North Tower of the World Trade Center. Forty-two minutes after, at 9:28 a.m., United Airlines Flight 93 was hijacked. It took only another twenty-nine minutes for passengers and flight crews to adjust their behavior. At 9:57 a.m. the passengers and crew on United Airlines Flight 93 assaulted their hijackers. Only an hour and 11 minutes elapsed from the first evidence of a regime change until the rational response was determined and implemented. It happened on a plane already in the air based on limited information obtained through a few telephone calls. Yet the response was no minor adjustment. It was dangerous and dramatic. The passengers and crew of flight 93 risked – and sacrificed – their lives. I find this very hard to reconcile with a behavioral view that people "are more like Homer Simpson than Superman."

Despite the joke about every four economists having five opinions, economists agree on many things. We agree that you are probably pretty good in your everyday economic decisions. We think you have little reason to invest a lot of time and effort in figuring out which economic policies will be the most favorable for you given that your vote counts for so little. For example: if you had to pay the 50% of the social security tax now paid by your employer, you'd probably correctly figure you'd lose some money. But economists figure your salary would adjust upwards (or less downwards) just enough that it wouldn't make much difference after a year or so. Are you going to spend a lot of time figuring out whether that is right or wrong?

By way of contrast behavioral economists seem to think that you are pretty bad at your job and at your day-to-day living. For some reason they also seem to think you are pretty good at evaluating the effect of different tax policies – and so will elect the politicians that will get it right. Well some behavioral economists anyway – a good place to conclude is with the writing of two behavioral economists George Loewenstein and Peter Ubel in 2010:

> … [behavioral economics] has its limits. As policymakers use it to devise programs, it's becoming clear that behavioral economics is being asked to solve problems it wasn't meant to address. Indeed, it seems in some cases that behavioral economics is being used as a political expedient, allowing policymakers to avoid painful but more effective solutions rooted in traditional economics.

Behavioral economics should complement, not substitute for, more substantive economic interventions. If traditional economics suggests that we should have a larger price difference between sugar-free and sugared drinks, behavioral economics could suggest whether consumers would respond better to a subsidy on unsweetened drinks or a tax on sugary drinks.

But that's the most it can do.

# References

Admati, A. [1985]: "A Noisy Rational Expectations Equilibrium for Multi-asset Securities Markets," *Econometrica* **53**: 629–658.

Ainslie, G. [2001]: *Breakdown of Will*, Cambridge: Cambridge University Press.

Akerlof, G. A. [2001]: "Behavioral Macroeconomics and Macroeconomic Behavior," Nobel Lecture.

Allais, M. [1953]: "Le Comportement de l'Homme Rationnel devant le Risque: Critique des Postulats et Axiomes de l'Ecole Americaine," *Econometrica* **21**: 503–546.

Andreoni, J. [1988]: "Why Free Ride?: Strategies and Learning in Public Goods Experiments," *Journal of Public Economics,* **37**: 291–304.

— and C. Sprenger [2010]: "Certain and Uncertain Utility: The Allais Paradox and Five Decision Theory Phenomena," Levine's Working Paper Archive 814577000000000447.

Ariely, D., G. Loewenstein and D. Prelec [2003]: "Coherent Arbitrariness: Stable Demand Curves Without Stable Preferences," *Quarterly Journal of Economics* **118**: 73–105.

Barro, R. [1974]: "Are Government Bonds Net Wealth?" *The Journal of Political Economy* **82**: 1095–1117.

Becker, G. and R. Posner [2004]: "Suicide: An Economic Approach," Mimeo, The University of Chicago.

—, M. H. Degroot and J. Marschak [1964]: "Measuring Utility by a Single-response Sequential Method," *Behavioral Science* **9**: 226–232.

Bernoulli, D. [1738]: *Specimen theoriae novae de mensura sortis* (Exposition of a New Theory on the Measurement of Risk).

Black, F. [1986]: "Noise," *The Journal of Finance* **41**: 529–543.

Blakeslee, F. [2003]: "Brain Experts now Follow the Money," *New York Times,* June 17.

Boldrin, M., L. Christiano and J. Fisher [2001]: "Habit Persistence, Asset Returns, and the Business Cycle," *American Economic Review* **91**: 149–166.

— and D. K. Levine [2001]: "Growth Cycles and Market Crashes," *Journal of Economic Theory* **96**: 13-39.

Bolton, G. E. and A. Ockenfels [2000]: "ERC: A Theory of Equity, Reciprocity, and Competition," *American Economic Review* **90**: 166–193.

Borgers, T. and R. Sarin [2000]: "Naive Reinforcement Learning with Endogenous Aspirations," *International Economic Review* **41**: 921–950.

Bosch-Domenech, A. and J. Silvestre [2006]: "Reflections on Gains and Losses: A 2 × 2 × 7 Experiment," *Journal of Risk and Uncertainty* 33: 217–235.

Brown, J. N. and R. W. Rosenthal [1990]: "Testing the Minmax Hypothesis: A Reexamination of O'Neill's Game Experiment," *Econometrica* 57: 1065–1082.

Bruhin, A., H. Fehr-Duda and T. Epper [2010]: "Risk and Rationality: Uncovering Heterogeneity in Probability Distortion," *Econometrica* 78: 1375–1412.

Camerer, C. F., G. Loewenstein and D. Prelec [2005]: "Neuroeconomics: How Neuroscience Can Inform Economics," *Journal of Economic Literature* 44: 9–64.

—, T.-H. Ho and J.-K. Chong [2004]: "A Cognitive Hierarchy Model of Games," *Quarterly Journal of Economics* 119: 861-898.

— and K. Weigelt [1988]: "Experimental Tests of a Sequential Equilibrium Reputation Model," *Econometrica* 56: 1–36.

Churchill, W. [1947]: Speech in House of Commons, November 11.

Cole, H. and L. Ohanian [2004]: "New Deal Policies and the Persistence of the Great Depression," *Journal of Political Economy* 112: 779–816.

Conan Doyle, A. [1893]: "The Final Problem," *The Strand Magazine*.

Constantinides, G. [1990]: "Habit Formation: A Resolution of the Equity Premium Puzzle," *Journal of Political Economy* 98: 519–543.

Costa-Gomes, M., V. P. Crawford and B. Broseta [2001]: "Cognition and Behavior in Normal-Form Games: An Experimental Study," *Econometrica* 69: 1193–123.

Cox, J. C., B. Roberson and V. L. Smith [1982]: "Theory and Behavior of Single Object Auctions," *Research in Experimental Economics*, Greenwich, CT: JAI Press.

—, D. Friedman and V. Sadiraj [2008]: "Revealed Altruism," *Econometrica* 76: 1, 31–69.

Dal Bo, P. [2005]: "Cooperation under the Shadow of the Future: Experimental Evidence from Infinitely Repeated Games," *The American Economic Review* 95: 1591–1604.

Davis, Douglas D. and Charles A. Holt [1993]: *Experimental Economics*, Princeton, NJ: Princeton University Press.

Dekel, E., B. L. Lipman and A. Rustichini [2001]: "Representing Preferences with a Unique Subjective State Space," *Econometrica* 69: 891–934.

DellaVigna, Stefano [2009]: "Psychology and Economics: Evidence from the Field," *Journal of Economic Literature*, 47: 315–372.

— and U. Malmendier [2006]: "Paying not to Go to the Gym," *American Economic Review* 96: 694–719.

Diamond, D. W. and P. H. Dybvig [1983]: "Bank Runs, Deposit Insurance, and Liquidity," *The Journal of Political Economy* 91: 401–419.

Dickhaut, J., K. McCabe, J. C. Nagode, A. Rustichini and J. V. Pardo [2003]: "The Impact of the Certainty Context on the Process of Choice," *Proceedings of the National Academy of Sciences of the United States of America* 100, 3536–3541.

Domar, E. [1946]: "Capital Expansion, Rate of Growth and Employment," *Econometrica* 14: 137–147.

Dufwenberg, M., P. Heidhues, G. Kirchsteiger, F. Riedel and J. Sobel [2011]: "Other-Regarding Preferences in General Equilibrium," *Review of Economic Studies* 78: 613–639.

Dusenberry, J. [1949]: *Income, Saving and the Theory of Consumer Behavior*.

Edgeworth, F. Y. [1881]: *Mathematical Psychics,* reprint [1967]: New York: Augustus M. Kelley.

Erev, I. and Alvin R. Roth [1995]: "Learning in Extensive-Form Games: Experimental Data and Simple Dynamic Model in the Intermediate Term," *Games and Economic Behavior* 8: 164–212.

Feddersen, T. J. and W. Pesendorfer [1996]: "The Swing Voter's Curse," *American Economic Review* 86: 408–424.

Fehr, E. and K. M. Schmidt [1999]: "A Theory of Fairness, Competition, and Cooperation," *Quarterly Journal of Economics* 114: 817–868.

Fiorina, M. P. [1971]: "A Note on Probability Matching and Rational Choice," *Behavioral Science* 16: 158–166.

Foster, D. P. and H. P. Young [2003]: "Learning, Hypothesis Testing, and Nash Equilibrium," *Games and Economic Behavior* 45: 73–96.

Fudenberg, D. and D. M. Kreps, [1988]: "A Theory of Learning, Experimentation and Equilibrium in Games," Mimeo, MIT.

— and D. K. Levine [1988]: "On The Robustness of Equilibrium Refinements," *Journal of Economic Theory* 44: 354–380.

— and J. Tirole [1991]: *Game Theory,* Cambridge, MA: MIT Press.

— and D. Kreps [1992]: "Learning Mixed Equilibria," *Games and Economic Behavior* 5: 320–367.

— and D. K. Levine [1993]: "Self-Confirming Equilibrium," *Econometrica* 61: 523–545.

— [1995]: "Consistency and Cautious Fictitious Play," *Journal of Economic Dynamics and Control* 19: 1065–1089.

— [1997]: "Measuring Players' Losses in Experimental Games," *Quarterly Journal of Economics* 112: 507–536.

— [1998]: *Theory of Learning in Games,* Cambridge, MA: MIT Press.

— [2005]: "Learning and Belief Based Trading," *The Latin American Journal of Economics,* 42: 199–207.

— [2006]: "A Dual Self Model of Impulse Control," *American Economic Review* 96: 1449–1476.

— [2009]: "Self-Confirming Equilibrium and the Lucas Critique," forthcoming *Journal of Economic Theory* 144: 2354–2371.

— [2009]: "Learning and Equilibrium," *Annual Review of Economics* 1: 385–420.

— [2012]: "Timing and Self-Control," *Econometrica* 80: 1–42.

— and Z. Maniadis [2011]: "Reexamining Coherent Arbitrariness for the Evalution of Common Goods and Lotteries," *American Economic Journal: Microeconomics,* forthcoming.

Gabaix, X. and D. Laibson [2001]: "The 6D Bias and the Equity-Premium Puzzle," *NBER Macroeconomics Annual* 16: 257–312.

Garrett, T. A. and R. S. Sobel [1999]: "Gamblers Favor Skewness not Risk: Further Evidence from United States Lottery Games," *Economics Letters* 63: 85–90.

GivingUSA Foundation [2009]: "U.S. Charitable Giving Estimated to be $307.65 Billion in 2008." Press release available at: http://www.givingusa.org/press_releases/gusa/GivingReaches300billion.pdf

Glimcher, P. [2002]: *Decisions, Uncertainty and the Brain: The Science of Neuroeconomics,* Cambridge, MA: MIT Press.

Godlewski, C. J. [2007]: "An Empirical Investigation of Bank Risk-Taking in Emerging Markets within a Prospect Theory Framework: A Note," *Banks and Bank Systems* **2**: 35–43.

Goeree, J. K. and C. A. Holt [2001]: "Ten Little Treasures of Game Theory and Ten Intuitive Contradictions," *The American Economic Review* **91**: 1402–1422.

Goldman, S. M. [1978]: "Gift quilibria and ParetoE Optimality," *Journal of Economic Theory* **18**: 368–370.

Graf, V., D. H. Bullock and M. E. Bitterman [1964]: "Further Experiments on Probability-matching in the Pigeon," *Journal of Experimental Animal Behavior* **7**: 151–157.

Green, D. and I. Shapiro [1994]: *Pathologies of Rational Choice Theory.*

Green, L. and J. Myerson [1996]: "Exponential Versus Hyperbolic Discounting of Delayed Outcomes: Risk and Waiting Time," *American Zoologist,* **36**: 496–505.

Grossman, S. J. and G. Laroque [1990]: "Asset Pricing and Optimal Portfolio Choice in the Presence of Illiquid Durable Consumption Goods," *Econometrica* **58**: 25–51.

Gul, F. and W. Pesendorfer [2001] "Temptation and Self Control." *Econometrica* **69**: 1403–1436.

— [2004]: "The Canonical Type Space for Interdependent Preferences," working paper, Princeton Economics.

— [2005]: "The Case for Mindless Economics," working paper, Princeton Economics.

Guth, W. and R. Tietz [1988]: "Ultimatum Bargaining for a Shrinking Cake: An Experimental Analysis," in R. Tietz, W. Albers and R. Selten, eds., *Bounded Rational Behavior in Experimental Games and Markets,* Berlin, Germany: Springer.

— [1990]: "Ultimatum Bargaining Behavior: A Survey and Comparison of Results," *Journal of Economic Psychology* **11**: 417–449.

—, P. Ockenfels and R. Tietz [1990]: *Distributive Justice Versus Bargaining Power: Some Experimental Results,* Frankfurt, Germany: Frankfurter Arbeiten zur Experimentellen Wirtschaftsforschung.

—, R. Schmittberger and B. Schwartz [1982]: "An Experimental Analysis of Ultimatum Bargaining," *Journal of Economic Behavior and Organization* **3**: 367–388.

Halevy, Y. [2008]: "Strotz Meets Allais: Diminishing Impatience and the Certainty Effect," *American Economic Review* **98**: 1145–1162.

Harrison, G. W. [1989]: "Theory and Misbehavior in First-Price Auctions," *American Economic Review* **79**: 749–762.

— [1991]: "Rational Expectations and Experimental Methods," in Gross, B. A. (ed.), *Rational Expectations and Efficiency in Futures Markets,* London: Routledge.

— [1992]: "First-Price Auctions: Reply," *American Economic Review* **82**: 1426–1443.

— and J. Hirshleifer [1989]: "An Experimental Evaluation of Weakest Link/Best Shot Models of Public Goods," *Journal of Political Economy* **97**: 201–225.

— and K. McCabe [1992]: "Testing Noncooperative Bargaining Theory in Experiments," in R. M. Isaac (ed.), *Research in Experimental Economics,* Greenwich, CT: JAI Press.

— [1994]: "Expected Utility Theory and the Experimentalists," *Empirical Economics* **19**: 223–243

Harrod, R. [1939]: "An Essay in Dynamic Theory," *Economic Journal* **49**: 14–33.

Hey, J. D. and Chris Orme [1994]: "Investigating Generalizations of Expected Utility Theory Using Experimental Data," *Econometrica* **62**: 1291–1396.

Holt, C. and S. Laury [2002]: "Risk Aversion and Incentive Effects," *American Economic Review* **92**: 1644–1655.

Hwang, S. H. and S. Bowles [2008]: "Is Altruism Bad For Cooperation?" Mimeo, University of Massachusetts, Amherst.

Ipsen, E. [1992]: "Krona's Fall Threatens a New Currency Crisis in Europe," *New York Times*, November 20.

Isaac, R. M. and J. M. Walker [1988]: "Group Size Effects in Public Goods Provision: The Voluntary Contributions Mechanism," *Quarterly Journal of Economics* **102**: 179–200.

Jones, L. E. and R. E. Manuelli [1992]: "The Coordination Problem and Equilibrium Theories of Recessions," *The American Economic Review* **82**: 451–471.

Kahneman, D. and A. Tversky [1979]: "Prospect Theory: An Analysis of Decisions under Risk," *Econometrica* **47**: 313–327.

Kandori, M., G. Mailath and R. Rob [1993]: "Learning, Mutation, and Long Run Equilibria in Games," *Econometrica* **61**: 29–56.

Keren, G. and P. Roelsofsma [1995]: "Immediacy and Certainty in Intertemporal Choice," *Organizational Behavior and Human Decision Making* **63**: 297–297.

Keynes, J. M. [1936]: *The General Theory of Employment, Interest and Money.*

Kix, P. [2010]: "The Truth about Suicide Bombers," *Boston Globe*, December 5.

Knight, F. [1921]: *Risk, Uncertainty, and Profit*, Boston, MA: Hart, Schaffner & Marx; Houghton Mifflin Company.

Kranich, L. J. [1988]: "Altruism and Efficiency: A Welfare Analysis of the Walrasian Mechanism with Transfers," *Journal of Public Economics* **36**: 369–386.

Kreps, D. and B. Wilson [1982]: "Reputation and Imperfect Information," *Journal of Economic Theory* **50**: 253–79.

Krugman, P. [1979]: "A Model of Balance-of-Payments Crises," *Journal of Money, Credit and Banking* **11**: 311–325.

— [2009]: "How Did Economists Get It So Wrong?" *New York Times Magazine*, September 2.

Laibson, D. [1997]: "Golden Eggs and Hyperbolic Discounting," *Quarterly Journal of Economics* **112**: 443–477.

Leijonhufvud, A. [1973]: "Effective Demand Failures," *The Swedish Journal of Economics* **75**: 27–48.

Leland, J. W. [1994]: "Generalized Similarity Judgments: An Alternative Explanation for Choice Anomalies," *Journal of Risk and Uncertainty* **9**: 141–172.

Levine, D. K. [1981]: "Extrapolative Investment Equilibrium," unpublished PhD dissertation, MIT.

— [1998]: "Modeling Altruism and Spitefulness in Experiments," *Review of Economic Dynamics* **1**: 593–622.

— [1999]: "Learning in the Stock Flow Model," in *Money, Markets and Method: Essays in Honour of Robert W. Clower*, ed. P. Howitt, E. de Antoni and A. Leijonhufvud, Cheltenham: Edward Elgar, 236–246.

— and T. R. Palfrey [2007]: "The Paradox of Voter Participation: A Laboratory Study," *American Political Science Review* **101**: 143–158.

— and J. Zheng [2010]: "The Relationship of Economic Theory to Experiments," in *The Methods of Modern Experimental Economics*, ed. Guillame Frechette and Andrew Schotter, Oxford: Oxford University Press.

Loewenstein, G. and P. Ubel [2010]: "Economics Behaving Badly" *New York Times*, July 14.

Lucas, R. [1995]: interviewed in "Economics Dynasty Continues: Robert Lucas Wins Nobel Prize," *Chicago Journal, The University of Chicago Magazine*, December.

Machina, M. [1982]: "'Expected Utility' Analysis without the Independence Axiom," *Econometrica* **50**: 277–323.

Majure, R. [1994]: "Fitting Learning and Evolution Models to Experimental Data," *Equilibrium Game Theory*, unpublished Ph.D. dissertation, MIT.

Mankiw, N. G. [1985]: "Small Menu Costs and Large Business Cycles: A Macroeconomic Model of Monopoly," *Quarterly Journal of Economics* **100**: 529–537.

— [2010]: "New Keynesian Economics" in *The Concise Encyclopedia of Economics*, available at: www.econlib.org

McFadden, D. [1980]: "Econometric Models for Probabilistic Choice among Products," *Journal of Business* **53**: S13–S29.

McKelvey, R. D. and T. Palfrey [1992]: "An Experimental Study of the Centipede Game," *Econometrica* **60**: 803–836.

— [1995]: "Quantal Response Equilibria for Normal Form Games," *Games and Economic Behavior* **10**: 6–38.

Mehra, R. and E. C. Prescott [1985]: "The Equity Premium: A Puzzle," *Journal of Monetary Economics* **15**: 145–161.

Milgrom, P. and J. Roberts [1982]: "Predation, Reputation and Entry Deterrence," *Econometrica* **50**: 443–60.

Mookerjhee, D. and B. Sopher [1994]: "Learning Behavior in an Experimental Matching Pennies Game," *Games and Economic Behavior* **7**: 62–91.

Nachbar, J. H. [1990]: "Evolutionary Selection Dynamics in Games: Convergence and Limit Properties," *International Journal of Game Theory* **19**: 59–89.

Nagel, R. [1995]: "Unraveling in Guessing Games: An Experimental Study," *The American Economic Review* **5**: 1313–1326.

Ochs, J. [1994]: "Games with Unique Mixed Strategy Equilibria: An Experimental Study," *Games and Economic Behavior* **10**: 202–217.

— and A. E. Roth [1989]: "An Experimental Study of Sequential Bargaining," *American Economic Review* **79**: 355–384.

O'Neill, B. [1987]: "Nonmetric Test of the Minimax Theory of Two-Person Zerosum Game," *Proceedings of the National Academy of Sciences of America* **84**: 2106–2109.

Osborne, M. J. [2003]: *An Introduction to Game Theory*, Oxford: Oxford University Press.

Padoa-Schioppa, C. and J. A. Assad [2006]: "Neurons in the Orbitofrontal Cortex Encode Economic Value," *Nature* **441**: 223–226.

Pedersen, L. [2009]: "When Everyone Runs for the Exit," working Paper, NYU.

Pigou, A. [1920]: *The Economics of Welfare*.

Plott, C. R. [1996]: "Comments on: Daniel Kahneman, 'New Challenges to the Rationality Assumption," *The Rationality Foundations of Economic Behavior* ed. K. Arrow, E. Colombatto, M. Perlaman and C. Schmidt. London: Macmillan and New York: St. Martin's Press, 220–224.

— and V. L. Smith [1978]: "An Experimental Examination of Two Exchange Institutions," *Review of Economic Studies* **45**: 133–153.

— and K. Zeiler [2005]: "The Willingness to Pay-Willingness to Accept Gap, the Endowment Effect and Subject Misconceptions," *American Economic Review* **95**: 530–545.

Prasnikar, V. and A. E. Roth [1992]: "Considerations of Fairness and Strategy: Experimental Data from Sequential Games," *The Quarterly Journal of Economics* **107**: 865–888.

Rabin, M. [1993]: "Incorporating Fairness into Game Theory and Economics," *The American Economic Review* **83**: 1281–1302.

— [2000]: "Risk Aversion and Expected-Utility Theory: A Calibration Theorem," *Econometrica* **83**: 1281–1302.

Rader, T. [1980]: "The Second Theorem of Welfare Economics when Utilities are Interdependent," *Journal of Economic Theory* **23**: 420–424.

Radner, R. [1990]: "Collusive Behavior in Noncooperative Epsilon-Equilibria of Oligopolies with Long but Finite Lives," *Journal of Economic Theory* **22**: 136–154.

RAND [1955]: *A Million Random Digits with 100,000 Normal Deviates*, The Rand Corporation.

Rapoport, A. and M. A. Fuller [1995]: "Bidding Strategies in a Bilateral Monopoly with Two-Sided Incomplete Information," *Journal of Mathematical Psychology* **39**: 179–176.

Roth, A. E. and M. W. K. Malouf [1979]: "Game-Theoretic Models and the Role of Information in Bargaining," *Psychological Review* **84**: 803–836.

— and F. Schoumaker [1983]: "Expectations and Reputations in Bargaining: An Experimental Study," *American Economic Review* **73**: 362–372.

—, V. Prasnikar, M. Okuno-Fujiwara and S. Zamir [1991]: "Bargaining and Market Behavior in Jerusalem, Ljubljana, Pittsburgh, and Tokyo: An Experimental Study," *American Economic Review* **81**: 1068–1095.

Rubinstein, A. [1988]: "Similarity and Decision-Making Under Risk (Is there a Utility Theory Resolution to the Allais Paradox?)," *Journal of Economic Theory* **46**: 145–153.

Salant, S. W. [1983]: "The Vulnerability of Price Stabilization Schemes to Speculative Attack," *The Journal of Political Economy* **91**: 1–38.

Sargent, T., N. Williams and T. Zhao [2006a]: "Shocks and Government Beliefs: The Rise and Fall of American Inflation," *American Economic Review* **96**: 1193–1224.

— [2006b]: "The Conquest of South American Inflation," working paper NYU.

Schelling, T. C. [1960]: *The Strategy of Conflict* Harvard University Press: Cambridge, MA.

Selten, R. [1967]: "Die Strategiemethode zur Erforschung des Eingeschränkten Rationalen Verhaltens im Rahmen eines Oligopolexperiments," in *Beiträge zur*

*Experimentellen Wirtschaftsforschung,* ed. H. Sauermann, Tübingen, Germany: JCB Mohr, 136–168.

— [1965]: "Spieltheoretische Behandlung eines Oligopmodells mit Nachfrageträgheit," *Z. Ges. Staatswiss.,* **121**: 301–324.

Shapiro, C. and J. E. Stiglitz [1984]: "Equilibrium Unemployment as a Worker Discipline Device," *American Economic Review* **74**: 433–444.

Sharkansky, S. [2002]: "Psychotic Death Cult Photo Album," in *The Shark Blog,* available at: http://www.usefulwork.com/shark.

Shiller, R. J. [1981]: "Do Stock Prices Move too much to Be Justified by Subsequent Changes in Dividends?" *The American Economic Review* **71**: 421–436.

Simon, H. A. [1956]: "Rational Choice and the Structure of the Environment," *Psychological Review* **63**: 129–138.

Sims, C. A. [2003]: "Implications of Rational Inattention," *Journal of Monetary Economics* **50**: 665–690.

Smith, V. L. [1962]: "An Experimental Study of Competitive Market Behavior," *Journal of Political Economy* **70**: 111–137.

Sobel, J. and L. Santos-Pinto [2005]: "A Model of Positive Self-Image in Subjective Assessments," *American Economic Review* **95**: 1386–1402.

Stahl, D. O. II, P. W. Wilson [1994]: "Experimental Evidence on Players' Models of Other Players," *Journal of Economic Behavior and Organization* **25**: 309–327.

Strotz, R. [1955]: "Myopia and Inconsistency in Dynamic Utility Maximization," *Review of Economic Studies* **23**: 165–180.

Sutan, A. and M. Willinger [2004]: "Coordination in Cobweb Experiments With(out) Belief Elicitation," Mimeo, Universiteit van Amsterdam.

Thaler, R. H. [1980]: "Towards a Positive Theory of Consumer Choice," *Journal of Economic Behavior and Organization* **1**: 39–60

Thaler, R. H. and H. M. Shefrin [1981]: "An Economic Theory of Self-Control," *Journal of Political Economy* **89**: 392–406.

— and S. Mullainathan [2010]: "Behavioral Economics," in *The Concise Encyclopedia of Economics,* available at: www.econlib.org

University of California, Office of the President, Student Academic Services [2003]: "Undergraduate Access to the University of California after the Elimination of Race Conscious Policies."

Veblen, T. [1898]: "Why is Economics not an Evolutionary Science?" *Quarterly Journal of Economics* **12**: 373–397.

Villaverde, J. and A. Mukherji [2003]: "Can We Really Observe Hyperbolic Discounting?" Levine's Working Paper Archive 618897000000000779.

Weber, B. and G. Chapman [2005]: "The Combined Effects of Risk and Time on Choice: Does Uncertainty Eliminate the Immediacy Effect? Does Delay Eliminate the Certainty Effect?" *Organizational Behavior and Human Decision Processes* **96**: 104–118.

Weber, M. [1958]: "Zwischenbetrachtung," in *Gesammelte Aufsaze zur Religionssoziologie,* ed C. B. Mohr, Tubingen, Germany.

Young, P. [1993]: "The Evolution of Conventions," *Econometrica* **61**: 57–84.

# Index

Adverse selection, 38
Allais paradox, 78, 79, 80, 10-12, 104,
    105, 106
Altruism, 30-32, 34, 36, 37, 43, 70, 74
American Airlines flight 11, 129
Anchoring effect, 81
Approximate optimization. *See*
    Approximate Nash equilibrium
Auction, 14-15, 67, 69, 122

Backward induction, 51, 60
Bank regulation, 37
Bank runs, 38-40
Beauty-contest game, 119-121
Becker-DeGroot-Marschak elicitation
    procedure, 81, 122
Behavioral economics, ix, 2-3, 5, 7, 66,
    77-80, 86, 90-91, 93, 95, 98, 99, 105,
    107, 112, 114, 123, 124, 127-130
Behavioral mistake, 90-91
Beliefs, 6-7, 24, 26, 64, 68, 111-116
    correct, 111, 113-115, 116
    incorrect, 78, 83-85, 112, 113, 114
    superstitious, 116
Best response, 29, 53, 67-68, 74
Best-shot game, 47, 53-55
Biblical game, 33
Bounded rationality, 18-19
Bus seating game, 33-35
    polite, 34

Code of Hammurabi, 115-116, 118
Coefficient of relative risk aversion,
    103-104, 106, 119
Cold War, 50, 52, 53
Commitment, 50-53, 95, 96
Common knowledge, 111, 119, 122
Competitive equilibrium, 15, 17, 18, 19,
    82
Competitive market
    clearing equilibrium, 17
Competitive markets, 6, 14-17, 58
Consumption lock-in model, 110

Continuity axiom, 101
Cooperation. *See* Altruism
Coordination failure, 44-45
Coordination failure equilibrium, 44,
    45
Coordination game, 43, 119
Crime, 22-24, 37, 86, 116-118
Decision node, 48
Deep Blue, 49
Diamond-Dybvig model, 40
Discount factor, 27-28, 35
Discounting 27, 29, 96
    geometric, 94, 95
    hyperbolic, 95, 127
Discrimination, 88, 89
    negative, 87, 88, 89
    positive, 88, 89
Dominant strategy equilibrium, 24, 33,
    34, 35
Drug use, 87
Dynamic programming.
    *See* Backward induction

Economic crises, 3, 83, 85, 96, 115
Efficiency wages, 83
Efficient-market hypothesis, 75
Endowment effect, 80
Epsilon equilibrium.
    *See* Nash equilibrium
Equity premium puzzle, 108, 109, 110
Evolutionary biology, 90
Excess volatility puzzle, 108
Expected utility theory, 80, 100, 102, 104,
    106, 107
Exponential growth, 11
Extensive form game, 56

Fallacy of composition, 22-25, 33, 127
Framing effect, 78, 79, 80-81

Game thoery, ii, 5-7, 14, 15, 24, 32-33, 38,
    48, 50

evolutionary game theory, ii
  *See also* Mechanism design theory
Game tree, 47-48, 51, 56, 61
Grab-a-dollar game, 47, 60-61
Great Depression, 45

Habit formation, 64, 79, 109, 110, 127
Hail Mary pass, 107
Harrod-Domar model, 45
Health club memberships, 95, 99
Health insurance, 37-38
Herding model, 86
*Homo economicus*, 1, 2, 5, 63, 94

Imagination, 91
Impulsive behavior, 97
Independence axiom. *See* Independence
  of irrelevant alternatives axiom
Independence of irrelevant
  alternatives axiom, 101-102
Inflation, 114-115
Information set, 56-57
Iterated dominance, 35

Kandori-Mailath-Rob model, 44

Laboratory experiment, 7, 30-31
Learning, 61, 128
  active, 113
  passive, 113
Learning theory, 59, 61, 63, 72, 77, 79, 99,
  112-13, 118, 119, 122
Level-k theory, 120-121, 128
Logistic choice model, 68
Loss aversion, 78, 80, 100

Matching-pennies game, 69-70, 71, 72
Matrix of payoffs, 23
Mechanism design theory, 15
Money illusion, 78, 83-84

Nash equilibrium, 6-7, 8, 9, 10, 12-15, 17,
  18, 24-25, 28, 29, 30-31, 34, 35, 44, 47,
  49-50, 59, 60, 63, 67, 68-69, 73, 74, 77,
  110, 117, 118-119, 120
  and learning, 7
  and randomization, 71
  approximate, 64-65, 77
  mixed strategy, 71, 72
  pure strategy, 29 43
  strict, 57

Negative externality, 25
Neuroscience, 123-127
Noise traders, 75, 76, 121
Non-cooperative equilibrium.
  *See* Nash equilibrium
Non-cooperative game, 5
No-trade theorem, 118-119

Overconfidence, 84

Panic, 125
  financial, 39
  market, 39
Pareto efficiency, 34
Payoffs. *See* Utility
Perfect foresight, 6, 17, 42
Perfect foresight equilibrium.
  *See* Competitive market
  clearing equilibrium
Pigouvian tax, 25-27
Pivotal-voter game, 7, 9-10, 66
Political game, 26
Poverty, 22, 86-87
Precommitment, 50
Present bias, 78, 93-97
Present discounted value.
  *See* Present value
Present value, 27, 29
Price stickiness, 84
Prisoner's dilemma, 33-35, 39, 43, 51
Prisoner's dilemma
  and fallacy of composition, 22-25
Probability distortion, 104
Probability matching, 124
Procrastination, 78, 91, 97-99
Prospect theory, 78, 79, 80, 102, 104-107,
  109
Public goods, 24, 47, 53

Quantal response equilibrium, 68-69,
  71-72, 74, 76
Quasi-hyperbolic discounting.
  *See* Discounting

Rabin paradox, 78, 80, 102-104, 106, 108,
  110
Rational expectations equilibrium.
  *See* Competitive market clearing
  equilibrium
Rational expectations model, 2, 40, 41,
  54

Recursive analysis. *See* Backward induction
Reduction of compound lotteries axiom, 100-101
Reference point, 104, 106-107, 109
Reinforcement learning, 124
Repeated game, 27-28, 30, 32
  and definite ending, 28
  and indefinite ending, 28
Risk aversion, 102-104, 106, 108, 109
Risk premium, 103
Rush hour traffic game, 12-13, 26

Satisficing, 64, 79
Satisficing behavior, 64
Schelling game.
    *See* Coordination game
Self-commitment, 94-95
Self-confirming equilibrium, 113-119
  and economic crises, 115
  and economic policy, 114
  and social norms, 117
Self-control, ii, 2, 96-97, 110
Self-fulfilling prophecies, 41, 116n.
Selten game, 48-50, 56
  elaborated, 56-57
Social preferences, 32, 82
  fairness, 32
  reciprocal altruism, 32
  spite, 59
Stackelberg game, 50-51
Strategies, 28, 34, 35, 49-50, 56, 69, 70, 74, 110
Subgame, 47-61, 67, 112, 114, 117
Subgame confirmed equilibrium, 117

Subgame perfect equilibrium, 47, 49, 56, 58, 61, 67, 113
  and robustness, 55
Suicide, 21-22, 128
Superstition, 115-118
Systematic bias, 85
  above average, 84
  emotions, 85
  limited attention, 85
  prior information, 85
  social pressure, 86
  understimate adaptation, 85

Torture, 11-13
Tough game, 35-36, 37
  altruistic, 35, 36
Transitivity, 23, 100, 101
Turing machine, 126

Ultimatum bargaining game, 57, 66, 113
Unbounded rationality, 1, 18, 19
Unbounded selfishness, 1, 2
United Airlines flight 93, 129
Utility, 22, 23-25, 33, 36, 39, 69-70, 79, 88, 89, 101, 102, 105, 109

Von-Neumann Morgenstern utility function, 101
Voter turnout paradox, 7-8
Voting theory, 7

Willingness to accept, 59, 80, 81-82
Willingness to pay, 17, 81, 86
Winner's curse, 69

Zero sum game, 70

# This book does not end here...

At Open Book Publishers, we are changing the nature of the traditional academic book. The title you have just read will not be left on a library shelf, but will be accessed online by hundreds of readers each month across the globe. We make all our books free to read online so that students, researchers and members of the public who can't afford a printed edition can still have access to the same ideas as you.

Our digital publishing model also allows us to produce online supplementary material, including extra chapters, reviews, links and other digital resources. Find *Is Behavioral Economics Doomed?* on our website to access its online extras. Please check this page regularly for ongoing updates, and join the conversation by leaving your own comments:

http://www.openbookpublishers.com/product/77

If you enjoyed this book, and feel that research like this should be available to all readers, regardless of their income, please think about donating to us. Our company is run entirely by academics, and our publishing decisions are based on intellectual merit and public value rather than on commercial viability. We do not operate for profit and all donations, as with all other revenue we generate, will be used to finance new Open Access publications.

For further information about what we do, how to donate to OBP, additional digital material related to our titles or to order our books, please visit our website.

OpenBook
Publishers

Knowledge is for sharing

CPSIA information can be obtained at www.ICGtesting.com
Printed in the USA
BVOW05s1053260214

346056BV00003B/61/P

"Seven dollars and forty-eight cents," repeated Jason. "That's not so much. You're really getting there, Benjy. Let me think about this."

Benjy was glad to let him. His own brain was worn out from thinking about it. He lay on Jason's top bunk and stared at the ceiling, thinking about nothing at all.

"If only I hadn't eaten all those fish I caught," said Jason, "we could sell them."

"You ate twenty-eight fish?" Benjy said.

"Well," said Jason, "some of them were kind of small."

Benjy was getting tired of looking at the ceiling. He glanced over at Jason's poster of Tony Trumbull charging through the line of scrimmage. There was no getting away from it—football season was almost here. He looked back at the ceiling.

"Worms," said Jason suddenly. "That's it! We can sell worms. Hey, Benjy, we'll rake in a fortune! Do you know how much they charge for night crawlers at the lake? A dollar fifty for this teeny little carton. And we can get them free in your father's compost pile."

Benjy could feel Jason bouncing up and down on the bed underneath him. "Wait a minute," Benjy said. "Hold everything." Jason's brain must still be

"I kind of hate to ask this question," his mother said, looking at the wagon. "But how was business?"

"Well," said Benjy, "I made fifty cents, three bunches of broccoli, a super-giant zucchini, around fifteen onions, a few red and green peppers, one Chinese cabbage, some rhubarb, an eggplant, and a few leeks. The corn is coming next week."

"Quite a haul," said his mother.

Benjy had a sudden thought. "Hey, Mom," he said. "Do you think I could pay for my mitt with vegetables?"

His mother shook her head slowly. "I really kind of doubt it, Benjy," she said.

Benjy started picking up the onions and peppers from the driveway.

"Yeah," he said. "I really kind of doubt it too."

# 10

>>>>>>>>>>>>>>

"You'll never guess how many fish I caught," said Jason.

Benjy didn't even try. He just waited.

"Twenty-eight," said Jason. "Bass and sunnies. And you should have seen the one I almost caught. That thing is a monster. It must be twenty-one inches long and it lives under my uncle's dock. It ate up around fifteen of our worms. Next year we're going to catch it for sure. We're going to use a lure. And I learned how to cast and we almost went fishing at five o'clock in the morning in my uncle's boat but his alarm didn't go off. So he took us out after dinner instead and he threw out the anchor and it got stuck on some rocks. My uncle had to dive down and cut it loose, only he couldn't find it and we almost had to stay there all night."

"Did you do anything besides fish?" asked Benjy.

"Nope," said Jason. "It was a cool vacation. What's been happening around here?"

"Nothing much," said Benjy. He told Jason about his toy sale and the vegetable emergency and Mr. Finelli.

"Too bad I missed the toy sale," said Jason. "I could have given you some great stuff. All I'd have to do is raid my brother's closet. He's never thrown anything away in his life."

"You're always saying your brother will kill you if you touch his things," said Benjy.

"Yeah," said Jason. "But he wouldn't even notice for about a year. How much did you make?"

"Almost seven dollars," said Benjy. "I could have made more, but I gave some stuff away."

"Not too bad," said Jason. "So now how much do you need?"

"Seven dollars," said Benjy, "and forty-eight cents." He'd counted it again this morning when he put in the fifty cents from Mrs. Bolton and his allowance.

on vacation. He leaned over the edge of the bunk. "Who would our customers be for these worms?" he asked. "Do you know anyone on your road who goes fishing? There aren't even any lakes around here."

Jason stopped bouncing. "Hmmm," he said. "You've got a point. I guess I thought I was still at the lake. Sorry, Benjy."

"The thing is," said Benjy, remembering again what his mother had said, "you've got to have something to sell that people want to buy." He frowned at the ceiling, trying to think of what it could be. It seemed like he'd already sold everything he could think of—lemonade, his old toys, vegetables. What else was there?

There was something. It had to do with something his father had said to him a long time ago, when he was just starting to go into business. Only he couldn't quite remember it. Everything was fuzzy in his mind.

He had to get his brain working again. Benjy focused his eyes on Tony Trumbull's gigantic leg muscles and thought. *Something to sell . . . something to sell*. That was it! The something he sold didn't have to be a thing, like a zucchini. It could be a service, like washing cars. His father had said you had to offer to do a job that other people didn't want to do—or something like that.

"Odd jobs," said Benjy out loud.

"What did you say?" asked Jason.

"We could do odd jobs," said Benjy. "You know, things that other people don't want to do. Like maybe weeding, picking up sticks, walking dogs. Stuff like that."

"Yeah," said Jason. "Watering plants, sweeping, cleaning rooms. You should see me scrub a sink. My mother makes me do it every Saturday. I'm an expert. 'No job is too big or too small'—that's our motto."

He bounced out of the bottom bunk.

"Benjy," he said. "This time you've got it! Whatever the customer wants done, we do it. It can't lose. We're going to rake in—"

"Don't say it," said Benjy, jumping down from the top bunk. "I don't care about a fortune. All I want is seven dollars and forty-eight cents."

"That's it," said Jason, grinning. "We're going to rake in seven dollars and forty-eight cents."

Benjy made a sign on a big piece of cardboard. In red letters it said: ODD JOBS MAN. Underneath he wrote a list of his prices: WEEDING $2.00, PICK UP

STICKS 50¢, CLEANING ROOMS 40¢, PICK UP ROCKS 50¢, WALK DOGS 35¢, SWEEPING $1.00, WATER PLANTS 40¢. At the bottom he wrote: BENJY WILKINS, 641-2250. HELPER JASON MCFEELY, 641-7690. THANK YOU.

He attached the sign to a stick so he could carry it. Then he and Jason got out his red wagon and loaded it with equipment—a rake, a broom, sponges, a bucket, cleaning powder, cloths, his mother's gardening gloves, a weed-puller, and a watering can. Benjy put in some sandwiches, too, so they wouldn't have to come back for lunch. They started down the road, Benjy carrying the sign and Jason pulling the wagon.

"Where do we start?" Jason asked. "Who's your best customer?"

Benjy thought about it. It seemed as if Mrs. Bolton was the one who had given him the most business. She was the only one who had bought vegetables and she'd bought lemonade and she probably would have bought toys from his toy sale if she'd been home. "Let's go to the Boltons'," said Benjy.

Mrs. Bolton opened the door with the vacuum cleaner in her hand.

"Adam and Jeremy can't play this morning," she said. "There's a big cleanup going on." Then she saw Benjy's sign. "What are you selling today, Benjy?"

"We can help with the cleanup," said Benjy. "We do any kind of odd jobs—sweeping, cleaning rooms, picking up things."

"No job is too big or too small," said Jason.

Mrs. Bolton looked as if she was thinking it over. Finally she shook her head. "Thanks anyway," she said. "But we can handle it. Adam and Jeremy have promised to help me."

Benjy could see Adam standing behind his mother. He was wearing an apron like hers and looking glum.

"Good luck, Benjy," said Mrs. Bolton. "And come back tomorrow. I might have some outside jobs then." She went back inside.

"Pssst," whispered Adam. "Benjy!"

"What?" said Benjy.

"I'll pay you to clean my room," said Adam.

Benjy wasn't going to fall for that in a hurry. "How much money have you got?" he asked.

Adam checked his pockets. "Ten cents," he said.

"That's not enough," said Benjy, pointing to his sign. "Cleaning rooms is forty cents."

"I've got more upstairs," Adam said. "I'll go get it. Wait here."

"He'll never find it," Benjy told Jason.

But in a minute Adam came back with two dimes, three nickels, and eight pennies. "Is that enough?" he asked.

"Yup," said Benjy, handing back three of the pennies. "Okay, you're on. If it's all right with your mother."

It was all right with Adam's mother—sort of. Mrs. Bolton didn't look too happy, but she told Adam he could clean up the playroom instead. When he heard that, *he* didn't look too happy.

Benjy and Jason went upstairs to Adam's room. As they opened the door there was a loud crash. A plastic sword fell down, just missing Jason's head.

"Booby trap," said Jason. "I used to do that so my brother and sister wouldn't come into my room."

But Benjy was staring at Adam's room. He'd never seen anything like it in his entire life. He ought to bring his mother over to see this. She'd never complain about his room again.

The floor was wall-to-wall toys. You couldn't even see the rug, it was so covered with trucks and blocks and Indians and space figures and Lincoln Logs and Benjy's robot and a ride-on Batmobile and pieces of games and broken racetrack and dinosaurs and racing cars. Clothes were thrown all over, on the bed, sticking out from under the bed, hanging from the lamp. All the drawers of the bureau were open. They were empty, and so was the toy chest.

No wonder Mrs. Bolton had decided to have a big cleanup.

"Forty cents to clean up this mess?" Benjy said. "It ought to be about four dollars. This is going to take us all day."

Jason was looking it over. "Stay cool, Benjy," he said. "I've seen my brother clean up worse messes than this. You just have to know how to handle it. Hang on, I've got an idea."

Jason went downstairs. In a minute he was back, carrying the rake and the broom.

"First thing we do is make a big pile," he said. "I'll do the floor. You do under the bed."

Benjy stuck his rake under the bed. When he pulled it out, he had a winter jacket, a stuffed monkey, three socks that didn't match, about a dozen Lincoln Logs, and a brontosaurus. He raked some more and got a sneaker, two more socks, three racing cars, some blocks, a pajama top, and a chocolate chip cookie. He tossed the cookie in the wastebasket and the rest on the pile.

"If this was my brother's mess," Jason said, "he'd sweep the pile into the closet and close the door. But

Mrs. Bolton might not like that. So here's what we do. I'll stand here, and you toss me a few."

Jason stood between the bureau and the toy chest. Benjy started tossing him things from the pile. A sock went into Adam's top drawer. A racing car went into the toy chest. Pajamas in the drawer. Blocks in the toy chest. When the top drawer was full, Jason closed it and started on the next one.

"Hey, this isn't bad," said Benjy, rolling two socks into a ball like his mother did when she did the laundry. "You can throw fastballs with socks."

He threw fastballs with socks and change-ups with dump trucks. He was just working on a curve with the pajama top when he noticed that the pile was gone.

"Look at that," said Benjy. "We did it!"

Jason shut the bottom drawer of the dresser, tossed a couple of leftover sneakers and boots in the closet, and sat on the toy chest to close it.

"Sure," he said. "Nothing to it."

Benjy looked over the room. It even looked good enough for Adam's grandparents to come and visit.

"No job is too big or too small," he said. "That's our motto."

"Come on," said Jason. "Let's go make some more money."

They waved to Adam on the way out. He was standing in the middle of the playroom, up to his knees in toys. He looked like he didn't know where to start.

"We ought to lend him our rake," said Benjy.

"Tomorrow," said Jason.

Benjy thought Adam would probably still be standing in the exact same place tomorrow.

They decided to try Mrs. Parkinson next. Since she was kind of old, maybe she could use a little help around the house.

It turned out she could.

"Odd jobs," she said, reading the sign. "That's just what I have plenty of. And Mr. Parkinson can't get to them the way he used to. You've come to the right place, Benjy."

She had them carry boxes up to the attic and newspapers out to the garage. They picked up sticks from the lawn and swept the front porch.

"Now," said Mrs. Parkinson, "if you'll just watch Muffin for a few minutes while I go to the store."

"Muffin?" said Benjy. Mrs. Parkinson must be cooking something in the oven.

"Don't you know Muffin?" said Mrs. Parkinson. She led them into the den. "Here she is. Here's our Muffin." A fat brown dog who looked like a rug was asleep on the floor. At the sound of her name her tail moved slightly, but she didn't open her eyes.

"She hates to have me leave her," Mrs. Parkinson explained. "She chews things. So would you boys mind just sitting with her? You can watch TV. I'll only be gone about half an hour."

Benjy looked at Jason. He shrugged.

"Okay," said Benjy.

Mrs. Parkinson turned on the TV. She brought them each a glass of milk and a cookie. Then she left.

"Speaking of odd jobs," said Benjy, "this one is the oddest. Imagine baby-sitting for a dog."

"Don't knock it," said Jason, stuffing his cookie in his mouth. "It's the easiest too."

He flipped the channels on the TV until a picture came on of a wagon train heading across the desert. Up on a cliff, though, Indians were waiting. "Oh, boy," said Jason. "I saw this one. It's cool. Only I never got to see the end. My mother made me go to bed."

He turned up the sound.

"Don't do that," said Benjy. "You'll wake her up."

What would they do if Muffin woke up and started chewing everything in sight?

"Forget it," said Jason. "That old dog's going to sleep all day."

Benjy watched her anxiously. Her side moved slowly up and down. Once her paws started twitching. He held his breath. But then they stopped. She must have been dreaming about when she was a puppy. He decided Jason was right. She was going to sleep all day. So he watched the movie.

It was just at the exciting part, where the Indians had the wagon train surrounded but the U.S. cavalry was on the way, when Mrs. Parkinson came back.

"How was she?" she asked.

"Uh—fine," said Benjy. He felt funny talking about a dog as if she were a person. "She didn't wake up at all."

"Now, let's see," said Mrs. Parkinson, reaching

into her purse. "How much do I owe you? There were the sticks, and the sweeping. According to your sign, I think that's a dollar fifty. And moving those things for me, and taking care of Muffin."

Benjy didn't know how much to charge for baby-sitting a dog.

"How about three dollars?" she said. "Does that seem fair?"

Three dollars seemed more than fair. It seemed terrific. "Thanks, Mrs. Parkinson," Benjy said. "Come on, Jason."

Jason was still glued to the TV.

"You can finish watching the program if you want to," said Mrs. Parkinson.

"We can't," said Benjy. "We have to get some more jobs."

He dragged Jason away.

"It's not fair," grumbled Jason. "I'm never going to get to see the end of that movie."

"The good guys win," said Benjy. "Hey, Jason, look how much money we got—three whole dollars. We might do it today. If we can just get a couple more good jobs."

"Okay," said Jason. "Let's do it."

No one was home at the Fryhoffers'. Or the Rosedales'.

"I know who we could try," said Benjy. "Mr. Finelli. He's as old as Mrs. Parkinson, and he's got that huge garden to take care of. I bet he could use some help."

Mr. Finelli was on his hands and knees in the Chinese cabbage.

"Well, if it's not my gardening friend," he said. "How did you like the vegetables?"

"My mother and father liked them," Benjy answered. He didn't think he ought to mention that the rhubarb made him sick just to look at and the onions and peppers set his mouth on fire. "Thanks again."

Mr. Finelli was reading the sign. "So now it's odd jobs, eh?" he said. "You're a busy fellow."

"I'm trying to earn money for a baseball mitt," said Benjy. "This is my friend Jason. He's helping me."

"Nice to meet you, Jason," said Mr. Finelli. "Well, as a matter of fact, I do have a job you could do. I was just starting some weeding. Usually it takes me about three days, but with you two helping me, I bet we could do it in one."

Benjy reached into the wagon for his weed-puller. "Where do we start?" he asked.

Pulling weeds wasn't as easy as baby-sitting a dog.
There were so many of them. It seemed as if they
grew better than the things that were planted on
purpose. And sometimes it was hard to tell them
apart from the things that were planted on purpose.
Benjy pulled up a baby carrot by mistake, and Jason
yanked out half a row of spinach before he realized
what it was.

"That's all right," said Mr. Finelli. "I was going to thin out those spinach plants anyway."

Pulling weeds was also hot. Benjy began to think about water—water in swimming pools, water in sprinklers, even water in a glass. Jason was thinking the same thing, it seemed. Benjy heard him muttering to himself, "If I was still at the lake, I could be swimming right now."

Finally Benjy said to Mr. Finelli, "Is it all right if we take a break?"

"Sure," said Mr. Finelli. He didn't stop, though. He was wearing a straw hat like Benjy's father wore, and he didn't look hot at all.

Benjy and Jason took a drink from the faucet next to the garden fence. Then they stuck their heads under it. Then they squirted each other.

Benjy felt cool. He went back to work.

But in a few minutes he was hot again. His legs hurt from squatting down. His fingers hurt from the weed-puller. And he noticed that he was hungry. They hadn't had any lunch.

"Would it be okay if we had a lunch break?" Benjy asked Mr. Finelli.

"Of course," said Mr. Finelli. But he kept going. For an old guy he had a lot of energy.

Benjy and Jason sat down under a tree and ate

their peanut butter and jelly sandwiches and their plums.

"This weeding is tough work," said Benjy. "Look at that." He showed Jason the blister on his right thumb.

"Yeah," said Jason. "This is one odd job I could do without."

"And we're just getting started too," said Benjy. "Look how much more we have to do."

They'd only finished four and a half rows. The rows that still had to be done seemed to stretch for miles into the distance.

"We'll never finish all that in one day," said Jason.

"Never," said Benjy.

Finally Mr. Finelli was taking a break. He took down a tin cup that was hanging from the fence and filled it with water.

"Well, boys," he said. "What do you think? Can we finish today?"

Benjy shook his head. "I don't know, Mr. Finelli," he said. "That's a lot of weeds."

Mr. Finelli took a long drink of water. "You know," he said, "I'd be so glad to get this weeding out of the way today, I'd be willing to pay you boys a bonus. What would you say to five dollars?"

Five dollars. Five dollars! Benjy did the arithmetic in his head as quick as a flash. Forty cents plus $3.00 plus $5.00. That was $8.40. Enough for the mitt. More than enough for the mitt!

Benjy looked at Jason. Jason grinned. They both jumped up.

"Mr. Finelli," said Benjy, "I *know* we can get it done today."

Benjy went to work like crazy. With his bare hands he dug down in the dirt after those weeds and yanked them out like they were his worst enemies. Looking over at Jason, he saw that he was doing the same thing. He and Jason were like the funnel clouds you saw on TV, Benjy thought, mowing down everything in their path. Or the people you saw in old-time movies, running around in speeded-up motion.

The bush beans. The pole beans. The leeks. The corn. The onions. Benjy did row after row.

He forgot about how hot it was. He forgot about his blister. All he thought about was the new Clyde Johnson mitt that was finally going to be his.

Somehow, finally, he was on the last row. And then the last pepper plant. And the very last weed.

Benjy straightened up. At least he tried to. He couldn't quite do it. He felt like a very old man. Older than Mr. Finelli even.

He looked over at Jason. Jason was just finishing his last tomato plant. He looked about the way Benjy felt. But he was grinning.

They'd done it. They'd weeded the whole garden.

"Well," said Mr. Finelli, "I've never seen anything like it. Once you boys get started, you really move. You did quite a job."

"It wasn't so bad," said Benjy.

Mr. Finelli reached into his back pocket and came out with a five-dollar bill. He put it in Benjy's hand. "Here you are," he said.

"Thanks, Mr. Finelli," said Benjy. He stared down at the five dollars. He thought he'd never seen anything that looked so good.

Jason punched him in the arm. "Hey, Benjy," he said. "It looks like you get your mitt tomorrow."

"It looks like it," said Benjy. "Finally."

He grinned and raised both arms like the heavyweight champ on TV.

# 11

›››››››››››››

"Twenty-two fifty, twenty-two seventy-five, twenty-three," said Benjy. "Twenty-three ten, twenty, thirty, forty, fifty, fifty-five, sixty, sixty-five, seventy, seventy-five, eighty. Eighty-one, two, three, four, five, six, seven."

He dropped the last penny on the bed. "That's it," he told Clyde. "Twenty-three dollars and eighty-seven cents. How about that? That's got to be enough for tax and everything."

Once more it seemed that Clyde gave him his goldfish smile.

"I agree," said Benjy. "Well, see you later, old pal.

When I get back, I'll have something to show you."

He dumped all his money into a brown paper bag and went downstairs.

"Are you ready?" he asked his mother. "Can we go?"

But his mother was still giving the baby her breakfast.

"Oh, no," groaned Benjy. "We'll never get there."

It used to be that his mother fed Melissa her revolting baby cereal. Now Melissa was learning to feed herself. Only it seemed as if she couldn't find her mouth. Sometimes she put the spoon in her ear and sometimes in her hair, and sometimes she tossed the whole thing over her shoulder. Benjy didn't think she was really that dumb. He bet if it was ice cream she wouldn't toss it over her shoulder. That baby cereal was awful stuff. But anyway, after just about every meal, his mother had to give the baby a bath. And the kitchen floor too. They'd never get there.

"Take it easy, Benjy," his mother said. "The store doesn't open till ten o'clock."

Benjy looked at the clock. It was only ten of nine. That was a whole hour. What was he going to do for a whole hour?

One thing he wasn't going to do was sit around

and watch his sister smear cereal all over herself.

"I'm going outside," said Benjy.

"Okay," said his mother. "I'll call you when we're ready."

Benjy went to the shed and got his old mitt and his tennis ball. He threw himself some high pop flies. But he kept dropping them. Maybe it was because he was too excited. Or maybe it was his old mitt. The pocket in it was really shot. And the leather was turning a whitish color, like it was all dried out.

It was the last time he was going to have to use that mitt.

"Benjy!" called his mother.

"Coming!" Benjy yelled back.

He raced to the shed, tossed in the mitt and ball, and ran to the car.

His mother was strapping Melissa into her baby seat. She looked all shiny and clean, as if she'd had not only a bath but a shampoo too.

"What time is it?" asked Benjy.

"Quarter of ten," said his mother.

"Oh, boy," said Benjy. "We're going to be late."

"We don't have to be there when the store opens," said his mother.

"No," said Benjy. "But I want to be."

He'd started worrying that maybe someone else

had been saving for a Clyde Johnson mitt, too, and this was the day that person was going to buy it and maybe there was only one left in the store. He had to get there first. Then he had a worse thought. He hadn't been to the discount store in three weeks. What if there were no mitts left at all?

"Could you just do me one favor?" he asked.

"What's that?" asked his mother.

"Drive fast," said Benjy.

She did go faster than usual. But then there was a traffic light and after that she got stuck behind a man driving a bulldozer.

"What time is it now?" he asked.

"Exactly ten o'clock," she said.

Finally she got away from the man on the bulldozer.

"Now could you step on it?" said Benjy.

His mother careened into the parking lot, her tires squealing. Benjy got ready to jump out.

"You can relax, Benjy," his mother said. "They're not open yet."

A little knot of people was crowded near the door. But the door was closed.

It would probably open any minute, though. "Just drop me off, Mom, okay?" said Benjy. "You can meet me in the sporting goods department."

"All right," said his mother. "Hang on to your money."

Benjy clutched his brown bag tightly. He sure didn't want anything to happen to it now.

He got into the bunch of people by the door. They were all looking at their watches and grumbling about it being after ten. He looked them over. Most of them were women with babies or little kids. He didn't exactly see anyone who looked like they were here to buy a mitt. You never could tell, though.

Benjy edged closer to the door. He stepped around a stroller and squeezed past two talking ladies. By the time the manager finally opened the door, Benjy was all the way in front.

He was the first one inside. At top speed he sprinted down the aisles. As he ran he noticed that the store had put up fall decorations. Maybe that meant they'd put away their baseball equipment. Maybe all they had now was footballs.

But when he got to the sporting goods department, there were the baseball mitts, just where they'd been before. Benjy saw the Doug Evans catcher's mitt and the Jose Lopez lefty glove. And, on the highest shelf, the Clyde Johnson fielder's mitt.

And there wasn't only one—there were three of them. Benjy reached up and took one down. For a minute he just held it, digging his fist into the pocket, smelling the genuine leather smell, tracing the Clyde Johnson signature with his eyes. This time he wasn't going to have to put it back. This time he could take it home.

After a minute he took down the other two gloves and tried them on. They both felt good too. And looked good and smelled good. Which one should he buy?

"So you found your mitt. Terrific!"

It was his mother, pushing a shopping cart with the baby in the little seat on top.

Benjy nodded. "There are three of them. Which one do you think looks the best?"

Benjy's mother looked them over. "Well," she said, "speaking as an amateur, I'd have to say they all look alike to me."

But Benjy wasn't so sure. He thought maybe the first one had a little deeper red color. But then the Clyde Johnson signature on the second one might be a little darker. It would be good to have darker writing to make sure it didn't wear off. But then there was the pocket. That was really the most important thing. He had to get the glove with the best pocket.

He punched his fist into each one. If only he'd

brought his tennis ball, he could try making a few catches.

"Benjy," said his mother, "I don't want to rush you, but you know what happens when Melissa stays too long in a store."

Benjy knew. What happened was trouble. She had about a ten-minute time limit and after that— watch out. He looked at her. Already she was wiggling in her seat. And her eyes were looking around. She was trying to figure out how to pull a few mitts off the shelves, he could tell.

He put his mind on the pocket problem. The first mitt still felt good. The second one was maybe a little stiff. The third felt good too. But the first one had that nice color. And the laces were good and tight.

"I've decided," he said. "I'm getting this one."

"Great," said his mother. She whisked the cart around, just as Melissa was taking aim at a stack of tennis ball cans. "Come on, Benjy. We pay for it up front."

There was a pretty long line at the cash register.

Benjy heard his mother sigh. He knew why. This was the baby's favorite spot in the store. There were always lots of sale things for her to grab near the cash registers.

The line went fast, though. Soon Benjy was handing the Clyde Johnson mitt to the cashier and watching her ring it up on the register. He had his bag of money all ready. He dumped it on the counter and started counting it out.

"That will be twenty-four dollars and nine cents," she said.

Benjy stopped counting. "Twenty-four?" he said. "Are you sure?"

It couldn't be. Twenty-two dollars and ninety-five cents plus tax couldn't be more than $23.87.

But the saleslady was nodding. "Five percent tax," she said.

Benjy looked at his mother. She wasn't paying attention because Melissa was just reaching for some razor blades.

"Mom," he said, his heart sinking, "I can't get it. I don't have enough."

"What is it?" she said. "Oh, the tax. I'm sorry, Benjy, I should have reminded you. On something that expensive the tax adds up."

Benjy looked at the glove and at his money. "I only have twenty-three dollars and eighty-seven cents," he told the saleslady. "I guess I'll have to come back."

He started putting his money back in the bag.

"Wait a minute," said his mother. "How much do you need?"

"Let's see," said the saleslady. "He needs twenty-two cents."

His mother reached into her purse and handed her the money. "That's not a loan, Benjy," she said. "That's a gift."

"Oh, boy," said Benjy, grinning. "Thanks."

"Don't mention it," she said.

Benjy dumped out his money again, and the saleslady started counting it. It took a while, since there was so much change. People behind them in line started muttering to themselves and switching to other registers.

But Benjy didn't care. He stood there with his eyes glued to his Clyde Johnson mitt and waited.

And then, finally, he was in the car driving home with his new mitt on his hand. This time it didn't matter how fast his mother drove. Benjy was happy just to feel the mitt on his hand and look at the Clyde Johnson signature and pound his fist into the perfect pocket.

The minute he got home, he called Jason.

"Want to come over for a catch?" he asked.

"You got it!" said Jason.

"Right," said Benjy.

Jason came over right away. He tried on the mitt and agreed that the pocket was perfect. "Can I try it?" he asked.

"Later," said Benjy.

They practiced pitching a few to each other. The Clyde Johnson mitt felt great. The ball zipped into the pocket with a little *plunk*, and it stayed there.

Then Benjy went out to the outfield.

It was the bottom of the ninth. The Yankees were leading, 2–0, on two home runs by Clyde Johnson. But the Tigers had two men on with two out and their slugger Ron Biggs stepping up to the plate. The count went to three and two. Here was the pitch. It was swung on and hit, deep to centerfield! Clyde Johnson was racing back. But it was near the wall. He'd never get there in time. It looked like a double, maybe a triple!

Benjy leaped up and made a desperate backhand stab. He felt the ball touch his mitt, but then he tripped and fell backward. He'd dropped it. It was a spectacular catch, but he'd dropped the ball. Clyde Johnson never dropped the ball.

Benjy sat up. He looked in his glove. There was the ball, sitting in the pocket like an egg in a nest.

He jumped up and held up the ball so Jason could see.

"Wow!" said Jason. "That was some catch."

"I told you this mitt was great," said Benjy.

"Yeah," said Jason. "Really cool. Hey, maybe I should get one too. This glove of my brother's is getting pretty old."

"I'll help you earn the money for it," said Benjy.

"We could do some more odd jobs," said Jason.

"Baby-sitting for dogs, cleaning rooms, maybe a little weeding."

"No weeding," said Benjy. "Anything but that."

"It's a deal," said Jason. "When do we start? How about today?"

"Tomorrow," said Benjy. "Right now let's play ball."

"Okay," said Jason.

And Benjy put on his new Clyde Johnson fielder's mitt with the perfect pocket and went back out to the outfield.